# FINGERS

versus

# THE MOON

## A SCIENTIFIC RATIONALE
## FOR AN
## EXTRA-SCIENTIFIC PSYCHOLOGY

## James A. Kline, Ph.D.

*Swan Mountain Press*

# TABLE OF CONTENTS

**\* \* \* \* \***

**TEACHINGS ARE**

**NOTHING MORE THAN**

*FINGERS*

**POINTING AT**

# THE MOON

# Chapter 1

## The Gall Midge and the Elk

The most difficult thing is to know
what we know and what we do not know.

**P.D. Ouspensky**
*Tertium Organum*

The cecidomyin gall midge is a remarkable creature. Depending on the availability of its normal food substance, mushrooms, it reproduces and develops by either one of two methods. When food is scarce, these small flies are hatched from eggs, and, after going through normal pupal and larval stages, emerge as sexually reproducing adults. The offspring are then free to fly off in search of their future.

When food is plentiful, however, reproduction takes a

1

somewhat more interesting form. Females reproduce by parthenogenesis, that is, bringing forth their young without being fertilized by a male gall midge. While this mode of reproduction is not that uncommon in nature, the gall midge supplies what to human sensibilities is a rather macabre twist. Instead of waiting to become adult flies, the reproductive females begin their motherhood in the pupal or larval stage. And, rather than emerging from eggs, the offspring develop live within their mother's body, literally devouring her from the inside out at they grow. In a few days they emerge from what is left of the carcass, leaving only an empty shell behind. But their days are also numbered, for in a few revolutions of the earth, their own future offspring will begin to devour them.

Prenatal cannibalism may seem, at first hearing, to be a strange, perhaps even poor, reproductive strategy. Yet it is extremely effective as far as the gall midge is concerned. When food is plentiful it permits an especially rapid way of increasing the gall midge population. Thus, when the local food supply is exhausted, there will be a large number of adult flies to look for new victuals. This, of course, increases the probability that at least some of the gall midges will find something to eat, which, in turn, enhances the probability that the species will survive.

The cecidomyian gall midge is not a creature that most people would consider elegant or noble, and its reproductive methods may seem distasteful or even repulsive to some. Many people would probably not consider it worthy of even passing attention. But the gall midge has managed to survive and thrive in an environment which subjects it to alternate extremes of both feast and famine. It has done so by evolving two distinct reproductive patterns which are optimal strategies for survival in the two different environment patterns it encounters. In an evolutionary sense, it has recognized and adapted to the "facts" of its world.

The Irish Elk, on the other hand, is the stuff of which legends are made. Although it was not exclusively Irish, nor actually an elk, it was indeed an impressive animal. With an antler spread of up to twelve feet and a body to match, it was the kind of parent that every prehistoric Bambi could look up to. Unfortunately, all we have left of this magnificent creature are a few sets of prodigious antlers, and a handful of bones, for the Irish Elk disappeared several thousand years ago.

Despite its impressive size and crown, this member of the deer family was unable to adapt rapidly enough to survive the environmental changes wrought by the last glacial period. We may never know for certain all the factors that contributed to this noble beast's demise; however, current thinking holds that the most probable primary cause was that its specialized evolution left it unable to adapt to the subarctic tundra of the glacial period or the heavy forestation that succeeded it. Natural historian Stephen J. Gould (1977) remarked that the Irish Elk was probably a victim of it own previous success.

How is this relevant to the field of psychology? The situation in the field of psychology is not nearly as stark as that of the Irish Elk; however, its commitment to objectivity and the scientific method in an attempt to achieve the same level of success as the physical sciences has unnecessarily narrowed its method of investigation. While the scientific method unquestionably has substantial strengths, the dramatic changes in ease of international travel and the explosion of information has made available frames of reference, ways of thinking and methods of study that were virtually unheard of in American psychology until the 1960s. I speak primarily of the concepts and methods of knowing that have been introduced to us from the Far East. The psychological principles found in Buddhist teachings and Buddhism's primary method of study, meditation, provide another body of knowledge as well as another method for studying human psychology. Just as the gall midge evolved two distinct methods of reproduction, modern psychology can now take advantage of two distinct approaches which can and should be viewed not as mutually exclusive, but rather as complementary.

It is probably not necessary to take as strong a position as Sigmund Koch (1969) - a psychologist commissioned by the American Psychological Association in 1952 to compile a status report on the state of psychology - who criticized psychology as "an edifice of ameaningful pseudoknowledge". But until recent years the psychology establishment has largely ignored psychological perspectives from other cultures, and has ignored the lessons from physics concerning the limits of science. While there are certainly dissenters within the field of psychology, in general there is a commitment to the objective analysis of the scientific method as the best way to increase knowledge. Nonetheless, Koch's conclusion (1969) that "The test of the Millian hypothesis [that the backward state of the social sciences could be remedied only by applying to them the methods of physical science, 'duly extended and generalized'] . . . has been fulsomely disconfirmed", still rings hauntingly in the background.

It is the purpose of the present volume to examine the methods of mainstream contemporary Western psychology, and to consider their strengths and weaknesses, particularly in contrast to the body of knowledge and methods of study of the psychology of the Far East. An analysis of any body of thought requires that one take the broadest possible point of view in order to make an unbiased examination. Thus, the current work is decidedly multidisciplinary in nature. And, although this book has a straightforward organizational structure, and makes an attempt to follow a logical progression, the reader should be aware that the presentation is one that, at times, challenges Western sensibilities. But such a challenge is an essential aspect of the prelude to a paradigm shift. One may recall that Galileo was forced to recant his heliocentric theory, and lived under house arrest for the last years of his life, though few now believe that we live on a flat planet which is the center of the Universe.

Questions regarding the accuracy and comprehensiveness of Western Psychology have come from within the discipline as well as from without. First on virtually everyone's list of those who have proposed alternative notions of consciousness would have to be American psychologist William James. His

*Varieties of Religious Experience* anticipated the issue before it was even recognized as an issue. Perhaps the most extensive contemporary critique was the six volume work, *Psychology: A Study of a Science* (1959-1963) by Koch. However, it was not the last. A very thoughtful volume by psychologist Michael Wertheimer (1972) addresses a variety of fundamental issues in psychology, among them the question of objectivity and subjectivity, and arrives at the conclusion that, ultimately, in psychology, the objectivist position has fatal flaws.

Robert Ornstein's *The Psychology of Consciousness* (1977) was among the first widely read academic psychology texts to explore the psychology of the East. He formulated the notion that there are two modes of consciousness - the logical, analytic mode of the left hemisphere of the brain, and the intuitive, holistic mode of the right hemisphere. Implicit in Ornstein's work is the idea that these two modes of thinking roughly correspond to Western and Eastern approaches to knowing. And, of course, who can forget the impact of Timothy Leary and his colleagues, Richard Alpert (later to become Baba Ram Dass) and Ralph Metzner.

There are so many thoughtful and relevant expositions from those outside the field of psychology that it would be impossible to list all the philosophers, linguists, physicists, religious scholars, anthropologists, and others who have had an impact on psychological theory. Among those whose work has had the greatest significance for this line of investigation are anthropologist and author Carlos Castaneda, physicist Fritjof Capra, religious scholar Huston Smith, Russian mathematician and philosopher P.D. Ouspensky, British writer Aldous Huxley, American author Alan Watts, psychologist Erich Fromm, and religious scholar Joseph Campbell. These individuals greatly broadened the frame of reference, and provided a basis for reappraising the appropriate scope of psychological inquiry.

Still, for many decades, conventional textbooks utilized in Psychology courses presented theoretical positions restricted to modern western European and American theorists - with the possible exception of Ivan Pavlov. Although this now seems unnecessarily parochial, there were not, for many years, any real alternatives in academic psychology. It is not that the writings of Eastern teachers have been completely unavailable. Alan Watts, Robert Ornstein, Charles Tart, and Herbert Guenther, to name a few, were exploring these writings which were rich with ideas about perception, conditioning, the nature of thought, concepts of self, and about what constitutes ultimate mental health. However, this body of work has generally been considered as religious and/or mystical, and it expresses ideas in ways that are quite different from the constructs of contemporary psychology. (A notable exception is the Enneagram which comes close to modern Western sensibility in its specification of nine types of personality profiles.)

Let me be abundantly clear that this is *not* a proposal that we simply dismiss the work of contemporary Western psychologists. Their work can be enormously helpful in understanding certain aspects of the human condition. Who, for example, would deny that much of our thinking and behavior is a product of conditioning, and that it is useful to understand the ways in which conditioning takes place. Or that it is valuable to understand the stages of cognitive development, or the elements of neuropsychology? The scientific method is enormously important to many avenues of investigation, and it would be fool hardy to think otherwise.

The good news is that it is not necessary to choose between Western and Eastern approaches to knowledge. Surprisingly, a key ingredient for the integration of these apparently disparate lines of thought comes from a source no one would have anticipated - the queen of the sciences, modern physics. Fritjof Capra's, *The Tao Of Physics,* (1975) explained the discoveries of modern physics and their relation to Eastern "mysticism". This incredibly thoughtful and insightful work provides a whole new framework which allows for an elegant way of integrating approaches to knowledge that had previously seemed to be mutually exclusive. Pioneering physicists such as Planck, Einstein, Bohr, Heisenberg and other physicists laid the groundwork for the ideas that have such important implications for the study of psychology as Capra's work intimated.

The widely held position that solutions to today's questions about human psychology can be achieved only through a greater commitment to more and more rigorous scientific research no longer seems plausible. As became apparent from the work of physicists during the twentieth century, the notions of reality on which scientific method was based had been compromised by the development of quantum theory and relativity physics.

In his biography, Einstein confessed that, "all my attempts to adapt the theoretical foundations of physics to this new type of knowledge failed completely. It was as if the ground had been pulled out from under one, with no firm foundations to be seen anywhere, upon which one could have

10

built." (Capra, p. 54)

In the same spirit of integration, Joseph Campbell, in one of his lectures on Kundalini Yoga, proposed that behaviorism, psychoanalysis and Jungian psychology could all be fit into this system of Indian philosophy. While Freud, Skinner and Jung might have raised objections had they been there, I was entranced by the idea that these apparently diverse theories could be included in a single framework without emasculating any of them.

While one might argue that there are still some unanswered questions and some details to be worked out, it is clear that there is a solid basis for reformulating our ideas about psychology. What had formerly seemed incredible, has become credible; an arena of mutually exclusive theoretical positions has been transformed into a constellation of complementary views on the totality of human psychology.

As Capra has demonstrated, following and expanding the lines of thought initiated by Einstein, Bohr and others, Eastern religious/psychological philosophies have begun to look surprisingly modern and insightful in terms of their description of the physical world and in terms of human psychology. The time seems ripe for Western psychologists to expand their frame of reference and to work toward integrating these ancient, yet modern, ideas.

In order to understand where we are, it is important to understand from whence we have come. Some of the older traditions in Western thinking such as Newtonian billiard ball determinism and Cartesian duality have certainly played a role in the evolution of our thinking. However, in addition to these more senior philosophical/scientific traditions, psychology has been strongly influenced by the cultural and scientific/technological trends which so strongly characterized twentieth century America and Western Europe. Consequently, the next chapter is devoted to examining the development of contemporary Western psychology in relation to the social and scientific context in which it evolved.

Subsequent chapters address relevant ideas from physics, biology, and language. The last four chapters are devoted to an analysis of current methodology in psychology, considering its Eastern counterpart, and to proposing a new model for psychological inquiry.

# Chapter 2

## Historical Perspective

At the time of its inception, psychology was unique in the extent to which its institutionalization preceded its content, and its methods preceded its problems.

**Sigmund Koch**
(1969)


An understanding of one's current situation can be greatly enhanced by understanding the events and circumstances that led up to it. Boring (1950), among others, has chronicled the history of psychology and laid out the path of its development in some detail. However, somewhat lacking in their expositions is a description of the social context of the nineteenth and twentieth centuries and their impact on this path. Reviewing what we know about the social fabric of this era helps to shed some light on why the science and practice of psychology arrived where it did.

If we look back at some of the pioneers of psychology we can see how they were products of their social context. Freud and his psychoanalytic theory were clearly a product of the Victorian era. There is little doubt that psychoanalytic theory is, to a significant extent, a reflection of Freud's own childhood experience. And these, in turn, reflected the culture of the late nineteenth century in Europe. Freud's recognition of the role of repressed sexuality so frightened his peers that his theory was rejected and reviled for many years. As a response to Psychoanalysis, Analytic Psychology was clearly marked with the mind print of Carl Jung, who was a product of the era that gave us other Germanic romantics, most notably Hermann Hesse.

Should it surprise us that American Psychology was equally influenced by its emerging culture? At the beginning of the twentieth century the United States was a land in the midst of a major transition. In just over 100 years it had risen from a small upstart colony to a nation that was on its way to becoming the pre-eminent world power. The effect of the industrial revolution was becoming apparent. The country was on its way to becoming an urban nation, and material goods were available in previously unimagined quality and quantity. There was virtually boundless optimism that Yankee know-how and determined effort could accomplish anything.

Contributing to the development of this new ethos were several threads, which, while conceptually distinct, were intimately interwoven in a fabric of mutual influence. One of the most obvious changes was in the way things were produced. Large factories were springing up all around. Goods could be produced more efficiently and in greater numbers where division of labor and assembly lines were employed. Craftsmen with a wide range of skills were gradually being replaced by workers with a specialized skill. As the size of factories increased, so did the degree of specialization and separation. Standardized and interchangeable parts, *and people*, increased the speed of the manufacturing process.

This radical change in the methods of production occasioned other changes in the fabric of American life. Not only were more products available, they were being produced at prices that many more people could afford. Mass production required mass consumption. Planned obsolescence and the shift from the philosophy of durability to that of replaceablility were necessary parts of this new scene. The country was excited about its progress defined as the abundance of material goods.

The other side to these developments was the impact they had on the way human beings were thought of. Life became more impersonal, and humans began to be seen as interchangeable parts. As population grew and clustered, bureaucracies emerged to deal with the increased volume of paperwork. Efficiency, production levels and profit margins replaced meaning and happiness as measures of success. If the lot of the average individual improved it was largely in the material sense, and was a byproduct, rather than a major goal of industry and the emergent society.

Closely linked with the growth in industry were the developments in science and technology. The rapid advances in these areas and the amazing breadth and diversity of their practical applications captured the imagination of the whole country. The introduction of electricity, the telephone, automobiles, refrigerators and indoor plumbing were all elements that eventually elevated the status of the scientist in the white lab coat to the status of high priest. It seemed that all the answers were at their fingertips, or else just beyond and waiting to be discovered. People looked more to science and technology and their objective methods for the solutions to their problems.

But perhaps the most notable events in the field of science took place outside of the context of the American industrial revolution. Just after the turn of the century, two remarkable intellects devised theories that were to turn the august science of physics on its ear, and make it a topic of discussion far beyond the academic scientific centers where it had long been cloistered. The culprits are, of course, Max Planck's quantum theory and Albert Einstein's theory of relativity. These world-shattering formulations and the resulting rapid advances in physics during the early decades of the twentieth century elevated physics to pre-eminent status in the field of science. It became the epitome of science and the scientific method.

Hovering in and around these developments, both causing and being fed by them, was a general predisposition to focus attention and energy on understanding and controlling the physical environment. It was an era in which the notions of conquering and harnessing nature to serve mankind was carved in bedrock. In Jungian terms, we were an extraverted nation, and our collective focus was on the external "objective" phenomena. Men of action producing practical solutions to practical problems were the heroes of the day. Contemplation, reflection and introversion were not in keeping with the spirit of the times. And one should not forget or underestimate the influences of the Calvinists and the Puritans. Such was the socio-cultural backdrop out of which modern American psychology was set to emerge.

American psychology finds its origins in the late nineteenth century, and its most famous progenitor is William James. (Ironically, the work for which James is best remembered is *Varieties of Religious Experience*.) James' influence faded as the twentieth century took off, however, and other lines of thought came to the forefront. At that time there were only two serious contenders for supremacy in American psychology, the Functionalist school, founded on the work of James, Thorndike, Hall and Cattell, and the Structuralist school exemplified in the work of Titchener.

Although psychoanalysis was beginning to make some headway in Europe, and was certainly debated in America, it was never really in the running for primary status among mainstream psychologists in America. Its method of long and expensive individualized treatment, openly focused on sexuality and the unconscious, was not in keeping with American sensibilities. Also, the subjective nature of the research methodology, and the use of concepts that were difficult to quantify, kept it from ever achieving any degree of popularity in academic psychology.

Structuralism, *the* psychology in its German homeland, probably never really had a chance in America. Brought from Wilhelm Wundt's laboratory, Structuralism was presented as a scientific approach to psychology. However, its choice of subject matter was immediate experience, a direct descendant of the German Phenomenological tradition, a tradition very much at odds with emerging American mindset. Partly because of its subjective, introspective method, partly because of the narrowness of the allowed subject matter, and partly because of the rigid and authoritarian personality of Titchener, Structuralism rather rapidly disappeared from the American psychological scene.

As has been noted by others, the Functionalist school of psychology was a coherent body primarily as a critic of Structuralism. Its pioneers included those with interests in animal psychology, learning theory, mental testing and statistics. They were united not by the subjects of their interest, but rather by a common interest in functional relationships, in empiricism, and in a pragmatic approach to the study of psychology. Though as a school, Functionalism died along with Structuralism, its founders had, in large part, determined the future direction of American psychology.

It did not take long for a new "school" to emerge. John B. Watson's Behaviorism was just the right psychology for the time. It eschewed the personal, the idiosyncratic and the subjective. It focused instead on observable behavior and scientific objectivity. It proposed a reductionistic and strongly deterministic view of human behavior. It promised a complete understanding of, and the concomitant ability to control, behavior. Its acceptance of the theory of evolution was evident in its willingness to accept as relevant to humans, data from rats and other animals.

Overall, Behaviorism fit almost perfectly with the spirit of the times, and was a natural as heir apparent in American psychology. Proclaiming as it did the ultimate mutability of behavior and the signal importance of environmental factors, Watson's psychology was clearly in line with the dominant

American predisposition to believe that any phenomenon - including humans - could be understood and controlled with enough scientific study and the proper technology. Watson (1913) outlined his vision in *Psychology as the Behaviorist Views It*. It was an objective, efficient, power-oriented psychology for an objective, efficient, power-oriented country.

Behaviorism was never the totality of American psychology, but it was the flagship, and most of the contemporaneously developing trends bore the stamp of its inclinations and patterns of thought. The increasing concern with the development of objectively validated measures, and the increasing use of carefully controlled research models and increasingly sophisticated statistical analyses bear testimony to this. The fact that the new psychology self-consciously modeled itself after physics in an attempt to approach the status of the queen of the sciences and improve its own image is pointed out in virtually every text recounting the history of psychology.

In and of itself, this direction of endeavor was not necessarily all bad. However, what psychologists seemed to have forgotten was that they were ignoring other legitimate paths of exploration, and involving themselves in something of an experiment. The fact that the methods of physics and other sciences had proven highly successful in producing advances in knowledge was certainly sufficient reason to experiment with their application to psychology;  it was not sufficient reason to install them as the only and unassailable basis of psychological research methodology.

Koch opined, as noted earlier, that the experiment was a failure; that history has clearly shown that most domains that psychologists study, "do not and can not meet the conditions for meaningful application of [the scientific] analytic pattern." He further contended that it is, "utterly and finally clear that psychology cannot be a coherent science." Most psychologists do not seem to believe that they were involved in an experiment, or that this experiment had had only limited success.  The approach that was stipulated into existence continued to grow and flourish with impunity.  Almost as a cultural vindication of the "truth" of positive reinforcement, the country rewarded behaviorists, and they increased their behaviorism.

Ironically, just as our predominant Western religion started with compelling ideas which, in some circumstances, became distorted and rigidified by unimaginative bureaucrats afraid of losing influence, who spawned the crusades and the

22

inquisition, Behaviorism acquired adherents who made a dogma of science in the same way that some of their religious predecessors had made a dogma of religion.

One reads in many introductory psychology texts that psychology has a long past but a short history. It was, unfortunately, this long past that was largely ignored as psychological science roared toward its meeting with manifest destiny. It is now time to step back and look more thoroughly and more thoughtfully at this long past.

The earliest recorded discourses on the nature of human psychology are now classified as religious, philosophical, occult, mystical or something similar. Yet the insights and value of this literature for contemporary psychology are becoming more and more apparent. Those who read it with patience, and make allowances for the unavoidable problems created by translation (not only from another language, but from a very different socio-cultural climate) can and have testified to its significance for psychology (see, for example, Watts, 1975; Ornstein, 1977; Goleman, 1983; Metzner, 1971; and Brazier, 1995). Modern physics, as expounded in Capra's work, has also substantiated aspects of these teachings concerning the nature of the physical world , most notably in the research on subatomic and celestial physics.

Lest we be too harsh on the founders of modern Western Psychology, we must acknowledge that there were understandable reasons for their choice to focus on the scientific method of the time. The impact of the cultural context was certainly profound. But there is a second, and equally important reason. The material on Eastern Religions which we now take for granted was almost inaccessible in America one hundred years ago. As air travel became a common experience, the world shrunk and familiarity with other places and other cultures increased dramatically. The forced migration of Tibetan lamas in the 1950s brought them to Europe and America. Zen masters and others schooled in Eastern religions followed. Texts formerly available only in Sanskrit, Pali, Chinese or Japanese were translated and became available to Western readers.

But access to this material alone did not mean that its value would be recognized and appreciated. Because much of it was originally written in languages that no longer survive, generated from vastly different cultures that existed thousands of years ago, it can be difficult to translate into a form that is easily understandable for twenty-first century Westerners. There are no books titled Psychology with chapters on learning, perception, personality, etc. Some of the teachings are in the form of stories or parables; others are more akin to philosophical discourses. Often, important terms have no easy equivalent in English. And as Fromm (1950) has pointed out, these systems often employ paradoxical logic in their expositions rather than the more familiar Aristotelian linear logic. Teachings such as "form is void, and void is form", or the doctrine of "no self" are often initially viewed by Westerners as nihilistic. The koans of the Rinzai Zen masters are easily misinterpreted as pointless mental gymnastics.

Yet those who, on the basis of a passing introduction to these ideas dismiss them as ambiguous, illogical, lacking heuristic value, or worse, might do well to keep in mind that physics, chemistry, medicine and many other systems of thought seem non-sensical to those who have not undergone the requisite education and training. The value of Eastern Psychology is not, however, undermined by the fact that the majority of people do not understand it.

There is yet another, more potent, reason that a discipline priding itself on an objective, data-based approach to problem-solving would be reluctant to embrace a school of thought considered by many to be a religion. Although a case can be, and has been made that science and religion are not intrinsically mutually contradictory, the historical record certainly highlights the conflicts between the two. Two of the most notable conflicts have been the Roman Catholic Church's suppression of the Copernican heliocentric theory, and the more recent Christian rejection of the Darwinian theory of evolution. But the heart of the difference has been the religious viewpoint that its core element is unquestioning faith in a supreme being, as opposed to science's generally atheistic, objectivist approach to knowledge. Then, too, the all-too-frequent accounts of religious leaders who have used their position to take advantage of their followers financially and/or sexually, have done little to confirm the notion that religion has an untainted path to the truth. It is not hard to understand why the founders of American psychology, and most who have followed, have rejected "religious" literature as source of principles and methods from which to generate an alternative approach to understanding human psychology.

Further, given the Western predisposition to separate and compartmentalize different disciplines, it should not be surprising that Eastern and Western Psychologies have entered into what might at best be called a very limited dialogue. Universities have a wide variety of different departments. This is a perfectly reasonable solution to a situation where there are vast differences among various fields in terminology, methods of study and goals. But it is also important to remember that life itself is not divided into departments. It is just life, and if we are to understand it as it is, we must be able to find a big enough framework to include in it all of the information we generate. While such an ultimate integration is far beyond the intention or scope of the present volume, it is hoped that the present work provides a contribution to integrating findings and concepts from apparently disparate fields in a way that enriches the study of human psychology.

# Chapter 3

## The Nature of Reality

Possibly, we shall know a little more than
we do now. But the real nature of things,
that we shall never know, never.

**Albert Einstein**

Over one hundred years ago, Max Planck and Albert
Einstein started a revolution that may have been, at the time, the
most overlooked (by the general public, anyway) and yet the
most important of the twentieth century. Their formulations
almost completely revised the ways in which physicists thought
about the physical world, time and space, and paved the way for

some of the most awe-inspiring developments of the modern era. Yet while most people now recognize Einstein's name, and can identify him as the father of the theory of relativity, few have even the vaguest notion of what relativity is all about. Fewer still are familiar with Planck or the quantum theory which he pioneered.

However, the findings of modern physics, which have shattered former notions of reality, have relevance far beyond the boundaries of that discipline. Certainly all those who call themselves scientists must take note of the fact that these findings have raised serious questions about research methods, called into question the formerly sacrosanct principle of causality, firmly rejected the ideal of a completely objective description of nature, and provided us with an example of one way of resolving the problem of contradictory data generated by the study of a single phenomenon. Psychologists, no less and perhaps more than, others interested in exploring the secrets of our world, need to acquaint themselves with the lessons of modern physics, and to reconsider the study of human psychology in the light of this body of thought.

The present chapter, then, is an attempt to present, in the simplest terms, the theoretical legacy of Einstein, Planck and their successors, and to point out the issues they raise for psychology. The presentation is necessarily general and basic in nature since a detailed exposition is beyond the intended scope of this work, and the level of expertise of this author. Fortunately, others have reduced the advanced mathematics and esoteric theoretical formulations to a conceptual level that makes these ideas available to those of us without specialized training in physics.

In order to facilitate discussion, the findings are reviewed under three groupings:

1. The structure of matter,

2. Conceptualizations of space and time, and

3. The phenomenon of light.

This structure is not implicit in the subject matter, nor is it necessarily the way in which a physicist would organize it. Rather, this structure has been selected because it best and most simply facilitates the presentation of the points salient to this discussion.

The search for the fundamental particles of matter has captivated human curiosity for thousands of years. However, only in the last century have physicists been able to carry out the kinds of investigations that have led to the current notions of the nature of the physical universe. The results totally contradict common sense (but so did the discovery that the world was a sphere) and have left physicists struggling to explain the new concepts in terms that an average person can understand.

That the atom (once believed to be the basic building block of matter) should turn out to be almost entirely "empty space" was hardly to have been expected. Yet the nucleus of the atom, which contains nearly all of the atomic mass, is only about 1/100,000 of the total volume of the atom. Capra (1975), in his excellent volume, proposes that if we think of an atom being expanded to fill the dome of St. Peter's cathedral in Rome, the nucleus would be the size of a grain of salt, and the electrons the size of dust particles whirling around it.

Our too, too solid flesh is not very solid after all. And, every second billions of subatomic particles, launched from distant sites, are zinging right through our bodies. Matter is so porous, in fact, that in order to make one of these particles (the neutrino) collide with something, we would have to place over 150 million kilometers of lead in its path. Indeed, there is so much space in atoms that if the human body were compressed to the density of the atomic nucleus, it would take up no more space than the head of a pin. The ancient Buddhist sage's dictum that form is void and void is form must now be viewed in an entirely new light.

The appearance of solidity is apparently a result of the high velocity (approximately 600 miles per second) at which the electrons move about the nucleus. According to physicists, they form a sort of cloud as a result of their great speed. The rapid pace of the electrons is slow, however, compared to the speed of the particles in the nucleus. These move at speeds in the neighborhood of 40,000 miles per second. Thus, matter which appears to the human eye to be solid and relatively quiescent, is anything but. At the atomic level all matter is characterized by intense, even frenzied, motion in what are relatively vast reaches of space. Yet it is this frenzy, harnessed by the great electromagnetic forces which bind the particles into a stable/dynamic package, that provide us with the appearances we take for reality.

As the search for fundamental particles became more and more sophisticated, the expectation that electrons, protons and neutrons might prove to be the stable indivisibles rapidly evaporated. With the eventual discovery of nearly 200 "elementary" particles, a strong suspicion has arisen among physicists that there is no such thing as a basic, indestructible, fundamental constituent of matter. While some particles are more stable and long-lived than others, all appear to be subject to transformations of one sort or another, given the proper conditions.

Further the once hallowed distinction between matter and energy is no longer. At least at the atomic level, this categorization has become meaningless. In his discussion of subatomic research, Capra (p. 50) notes that, "matter has appeared in these experiments to be completely mutable. All particles can be transmuted into other particles; they can be created from energy and vanish into energy."

But perhaps the most astonishing discovery was that matter is created out of, and disappears into, the vacuum of "empty space." In Capra's words, "The distinction between matter and empty space finally had to be abandoned when it became evident that virtual particles can come into being spontaneously out of the void, and vanish again into the void . . . The vacuum is far from empty. On the contrary, it contains an unlimited number of particles which come into being and vanish without end."

With the development of quantum field theories, even the

classical contrast between particles and the space surrounding them broke down. "The quantum field is [now] seen as the fundamental physical entity; a continuous medium which is present everywhere in space." (Capra, p. 210) In the words of Albert Einstein, "We may therefore regard matter as being constituted by the region of space in which the field is extremely intense . . . There is no place in this new kind of physics for both field and matter, for the field is the only reality." (Capra, p. 211)

And Herman Weyl (1949) writes, "According to the [field theory of matter] a material particle such as an electron is merely a small domain of the electrical field within which the field strength assumes enormously high values, indicating that a comparatively huge field of energy is concentrated in a very small space. Such an energy knot, which is by no means clearly delineated against the remaining field, propagates through empty space like a water wave across the surface of a lake; there is no such thing as one and the same substance of which an electron consists at all times." (Capra, p. 213)

Another unexpected and problematical finding for physicists was the discovery that, "Subatomic particles do not exist with certainty at definite places, but rather show 'tendencies to exist', and atomic events do not occur with certainty at definite times and in definite ways, but rather show 'tendencies to occur.' . . . In quantum theory we came to recognize probability as a fundamental feature of the atomic reality which governs all processes, and even the existence, of matter." (Capra, p.133)

So, if we are to believe the physicists, we live in a physical world whose actuality completely belies our senses and our common sense. What seems so solid is almost entirely empty space; what we thought was empty space is actually a field of mutable energy/mass in which particles continually appear and disappear; particles are not really particles at all, and we can't locate them with any certainty, we can only say where they are likely to be. All our conventional notions of the nature of physical reality have to be given up.

And there is yet another consideration. Our environment represents only one organizational pattern of matter. "When thermal energy increases about a hundred fold, as it does in most stars, all atomic and molecular structures are destroyed." (Capra, p. 74) Thus, most of the matter in the universe exists in a state that is very different from the state it assumes in our immediate life space.

Another victim of this line of research was the principle of causality. While it is (and will no doubt continue to be) a very useful convention in the description of events in our daily lives, it appears to have limited, if any, applicability at the subatomic level. The renowned Danish physicist, Niels Bohr wrote, "Planck's discovery of the elementary quantum of action . . . has brought about a complete revision of the foundations underlying our description of natural phenomena." (Bohr, 1934, p. 92)

A result of the application of Planck's discovery and the development of quantum theory has been, "the renunciation of the causal space-time mode of description that characterizes the classical physical theories which have experienced such a profound clarification through the theory of relativity." (Bohr, p. 92)

Regarding the disintegration of the atomic nuclei of radioactive elements, Bohr observes that, "so far as we are able to judge from all evidence, [this takes] place without any external cause." This is, in his words, a "peculiar failure of the causal mode of description." ( p. 104) He goes on to say that, "Indeed, only by a conscious resignation of our usual demands for visualization and causality was it possible to make Planck's discovery fruitful in explaining the properties of the elements on the basis of our knowledge of the building stones of atoms." (p. 108) Further, "we must consider this renunciation as an essential advance in our understanding." (p. 115) Bohr concludes that, "We are . . . so far removed from a causal description that an atom in a stationary state may, in general, even be said to possess a free choice between various possible transitions to other states." (p. 109)

Bohr's sentiments are echoed by Louis de Broglie, another pioneer, who commented that the subatomic world appears to be, "governed by statistical laws and not by any causal mechanisms." (from Clark, 1971, p. 338) This does not mean that there is no order at the subatomic level; rather that, given our current research techniques, we are unable to verify causal relations in our conventional sense of the term.

A second realm in which the new physics has given us a new view of reality is that of time and space. Einstein's theory of relativity broke open the way for a drastic revision in previous conceptions. Classical physics was founded on the notion of a three dimensional space (describable in terms of Euclidian geometry) in which physical objects had a certain objectively real existence apart from any observer or observations made upon them. Time was conceived as a dimension separate from the physical world which "flowed along" at a constant rate.

Relativity proposed, and subsequent research confirmed, however, that this classical view was incorrect in several important respects. For one thing, it was discovered that material objects do not have a single unique objective existence. Rather, one's judgment of the dimensional properties of an object depends on one's motion relative to the object. As Capra has noted, "in classical physics it was always assumed that rods in motion and at rest would have the same length. Relativity theory has shown that this is not true. The length of an object depends on its motion relative to the observer and it changes with the velocity of that motion. The change is such that the object contracts in the direction of the motion . . . It becomes shorter with increasing velocity relative to the observer." ( p. 70)

The same relative situation applies to time. How one orders events in time depends on how rapidly one is moving in relation to the observed events. Thus, two events that appear simultaneous to the viewer may occur in different temporal sequences to other observers moving at different relative velocities. Another aspect of relative time is that as relative speed increases, time slows down. Thus we have the classic (hypothetical, but verifiable) case of one of a pair of identical twins returning from a fast round trip into outer space exiting her space ship younger than her sister who remained on Earth.

At speeds of low magnitude relative to the speed of light, the effects noted above are negligible, and in most common situations may be ignored. However, as relative speed approaches the speed of light, the effects become measurable and significant. And, whether we remember it or not when driving to the grocery store, the universe is a relativistic one.

It has also been predicted and confirmed that both space and time are affected by gravitational fields. Three dimensional space is bent by strong gravitational fields. Thus, the space of the universe is curved. Exactly what this means in an experiential sense, no one has been able to state concisely in simple English. Nonetheless, the phenomenon, as understood by physicists, must be taken into account in many astronomical calculations.

Time is likewise affected by the gravitational effects that curve space. Time "slows down" in the presence of strong gravitational fields. This phenomenon is most fascinatingly illustrated by a consideration of the flow of events on a collapsing star. As a star collapses in on itself, it becomes more and more dense, and the strength of its gravitational field increases substantially. Eventually, the field becomes so strong that nothing, not even light, can escape from the surface of the star. At this point the star becomes invisible to observers. This marks the birth of what have come to be called black holes.

The strong gravitational field which dramatically curves the surrounding space and eventually prevents the escape of light, also has a peculiar effect on time. "To an outside observer, the flow of time on the star's surface slows down as the star collapses, and it stops altogether when [the gravitational field becomes strong enough to prevent light from escaping]. Therefore, [to an outside observer] the complete collapse of the star takes an infinite time. [On the star, however], time continues to flow normally and the collapse is completed after a finite period of time." (Capra, p. 178)

Perhaps the most difficult aspect of relativity to grasp is the notion of space-time. No longer is time treated as a phenomenon separate from space; instead space is conceived of as four dimensional, with time being the fourth dimension. Saying this is one thing, understanding it is another. The difficulty, as Capra points out, is that, "All these relativistic effects only seem strange because we cannot experience the

41

four dimensional space-time world with our senses, but can only observe its three dimensional images. . . . If we could visualize the four-dimensional space-time reality, there would be nothing paradoxical about it." (Capra, p. 171)

Physicist Louis de Broglie begins to sound like a mystic in his discussion of the problem. "In space-time, everything which for each of us constitutes the past, the present, and the future is given *en bloc* . . . Each observer, as his time passes, discovers, so to speak, new slices of space-time which appear to him as successive aspects of the material world, though in reality, the ensemble of events constituting space-time exist prior to his knowledge of them." (Capra, p. 185)

Due to the nature of the problem, direct apperception of space-time is impossible - at least in our normal mode of consciousness. An interesting analogical approach to the understanding of space-time is, however, provided for us in P.D. Ouspensky's (1945) stimulating volume, *Tertium Organum.* Ouspensky proposes that we consider the life and experience of a two dimensional being, i.e., a being who lives in a plane. As Ouspensky demonstrates, this exercise provides us with some thought-provoking conceptual tools for the consideration of space-time.

According to Ouspensky, "The two dimensional being will regard straight lines only as immobile matter; irregular lines and curves will seem to him moving. So far as really moving lines are concerned, that is lines [formed by] planes [of solids] passing through or moving along [our two-dimensional being's plane] he probably will regard them as living beings. He will affirm that there is something in them which differentiates them from other bodies; vital energy or even a soul." (p.. 55) That is because, to a two-dimensional being, three dimensional objects and movement along the axis of the third dimension are inconceivable.

"If a multi-colored cube passes through the plane, the plane being will perceive the entire cube and its motion as a change in color of lines lying in the plane. Thus, if a blue line replaces a red one, the plane being will regard the red line as a past event. . . . For a being living in a [horizontal] plane, everything above and below the plane will be existing in time." ( p.. 56)

"If we pass a spiral up through the [plane], the intersection will give a point moving in a circle (shown by the dotted line in Figure 1.). For the plane being, such a point, moving in a circle in its plane would probably constitute a cosmical phenomenon, something like the motion of a planet in its orbit." ( p. 61)

"Having no idea of the phenomenon proceeding outside of the plane . . . the plane being will think of all phenomena as proceeding on his plane . . . [and] he will consider [them] as being in causal interdependence, one with another; that is, he will think that one phenomenon is the effect of another which has happened right there." ( p. 56)

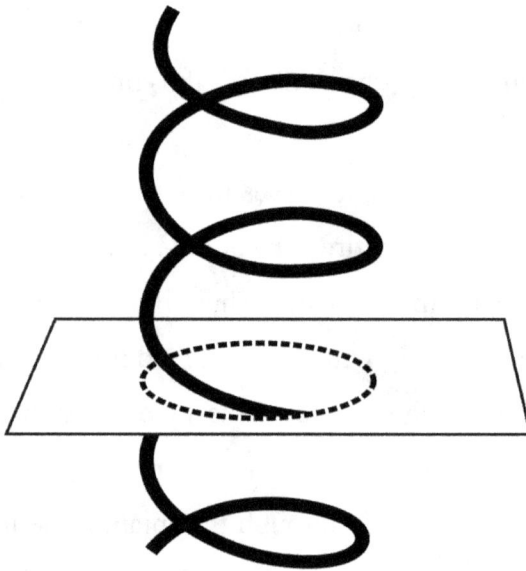

*Figure 1*

"Thus we may say that the idea of time is bound up with the idea of causation and functional interdependence. Without time, causation cannot exist, just as without time, motion or the absence of motion cannot exist." (p 33)

Returning to the problem of three-dimensional beings, Ouspensky says, "Four dimensional space, if we try to imagine it to ourselves, will be the infinite repetition of our space, of our infinite three dimensional sphere, as a line is the infinite repetition of a point. . . . We are in error in thinking that that three dimensional body is, in itself, something real. It is the *projection* of the four dimensional body - its picture - the image of it on our plane." (p. 45)

This three dimensional cross-section, then, actually extends in a direction not confined in it, i.e., into the fourth dimension. The four-dimensional body may be conceived, "as an infinite number of three-dimensional bodies [just as four-dimensional space may be conceived of] as an infinite number of three-dimensional spaces." (Ouspensky, p. 29)

Just as we can see and understand things in a way that is completely beyond the scope of the two-dimensional being, we must ask ourselves what reality lies beyond the range of our limited three-dimensional understanding.

Offering us a parting shot, Ouspensky proposes that, "extension in time is extension into unknown space, and therefore time is the fourth dimension of space. . . . And, in reality, eternity is not the infinite dimension of time, but the one perpendicular to time." (p. 40)

The third aspect of modern physics important to our discussion is light. The nature of light has long been a subject of conjecture among students of nature. Early in the current century, physicists were divided into two camps, each with a different view of how light was propagated. The solution which finally emerged is the result of an interesting compromise.

Early research on the nature of light had shown puzzling and contradictory results. On the one hand, it had been shown that ultraviolet light directed at the surface of certain metals could knock electrons out of that metal. This was labeled the photoelectric effect, and suggested that light must consist of moving particles. On the other hand, interference patterns known to be associated with wave phenomena were found when two light sources of different intensities were examined at the point where they converged. Thus, there was convincing evidence that light consisted of particles, and equally convincing evidence that it was composed of waves.

The dilemma remained unresolved for some time until Niels Bohr landed on the idea of complementarity. In his solution, Bohr proposed that the true nature of light is yet beyond our ken, but, that in certain circumstances it behaves as if it were particles, in others as if it were waves. Each theory is therefore correct in a limited sense, and both must be retained.

As well a providing a most satisfactory solution to the existing problem, Bohr's principle of complementarity pointed up an important fact. *The way in which one sets up an experiment is crucial in determining what one will find.* And, the result of one experiment does not necessarily exclude the findings of a differently designed experiment. In the end, what seemed like a clear either/or situation was finally solved by a both/and solution. As will be clear at a later point, it is less the truth about the nature of light that is of interest here, than it is the way in which apparently contradictory data were handled, and a satisfactory solution defined.

So what lessons can we learn from this esoteric set of research findings and ideas? Beyond the fascinating revision of the reality behind what our senses tell us, there are several important considerations that deserve our attention. First, we don't, and can't, know the real truth about what makes up our world, at least not using the ideas and methods of study so far developed by modern science. Nature has created us through the evolutionary process to equip us optimally for survival in a tightly circumscribed niche. But the very specialization which allows us to thrive in our niche, also confers limitations. The development and refinement of the very senses that enhance our chances of survival in our particular sphere has also limited our ability to experience and understand phenomena that lie outside that sphere. It appears that we must concur with Einstein that we shall never know the real nature of our universe.

Second, not only are we limited by the degree of our specialization, in a very fundamental sense we are the creators as much as we are the discoverers of our world. Physicist Geoffery Chew took this idea to its logical, if controversial, conclusion in his Bootstrap Hypothesis. Chew proposed that not only are there no fundamental constituents of matter, but that there are likewise no fundamental laws, principles or equations inherent in the structure of the universe. Rather, he suggested, all principles, laws and equations are the creative productions of the human mind.

Chew's hypothesis, regarded by some as somewhat over-ambitious, follows, at least in part, from the recognition of a methodological problem in atomic physics, namely that the properties of a particle under study cannot be defined independently of the processes of preparation and measurement. If either of these are changed, the properties of the particle change also. How we design our experiments and measure phenomena determine what we will find.

As Niels Bohr (1934) so eloquently put it, "there is no question of a failure of the fundamental principles of science within the domain where we could justly expect them to apply. The discovery of the quantum of action shows us, in fact, not only the natural limitation of classical physics, but, by throwing a new light upon the old philosophical problem of the objective existence of phenomena independently of our observations, confronts us with a situation hitherto unknown in natural science." (p. 115)

Third, the notion of causality must be viewed in a new light. While the failure of physicists to discover causal relations at the subatomic level does not mean that they do not exist there, it does mean that causality as a universal principle cannot be proved, and we must view it as an hypotheses, albeit a very useful one in some contexts. If everything past, present and future always exists as de Broglie claims, either we must completely rework the concept or throw it out altogether.

Fourth, there is an important lesson to be learned from Bohr's principle of complementarity. That lesson is that when we have contradictory data or theories about a given phenomenon, the "true" nature of that phenomenon is not necessarily completely represented by either one or the other position, but may be very different than either, yet inclusive of both. (The free will vs. determinism problem may well be another example of such an apparently irreconcilable conflict.) Both theories of the nature of light have their sphere of usefulness regardless of whether either represents the ultimate truth.

Finally, we learn something important from the way in which quantum/relativity physics superseded Newtonian physics. As long as human interest and attention was focused on the "middle range" of physical phenomena, classical physics was (and still is) perfectly adequate. However, as curiosity and research began to penetrate the mysteries of the atom on the one hand, and the vast distances of outer space on the other, it became clear that new models were needed to adequately understand the new data. The new theories did not eliminate classical physics, they merely provided a bigger container in which to place those laws. As Bohr noted, the classical theories will never become superfluous because "higher" physics in some important ways, e.g., the process of measurement, still depends on classical physics. Still, nowhere is it more clear than in the field of physics that the map is not the territory.

In a very interesting recent work, physicist Lee Smolin (2006) reflects that in the two hundred years leading up to 1981 physics had enjoyed explosive growth - new ideas and theories that produced hypotheses that were tested and confirmed. But in the early 1980s, he observes, things ground to a halt. Since then, he remarks, "when it comes to extending our knowledge of the laws of nature, we have made no real progress".

Not that physicists have been idle. Over the last three decades theorists have proposed at least a dozen new approaches, the most popular being string theory. It proposes to describe both gravity and elementary particles, and asserts the presence of as yet undetected dimensions and additional elementary particles - all of which arise from the vibrations of a single entity - a string. However, string theory appears to exist in a virtually infinite number of versions, and, so far, there is little empirical evidence to support it/them. Current attempts to create/observe the Higgs Boson may shed some light on the fundamental nature of energy/matter. It is not without a certain amount of paradoxical humor that I say that only time will tell.

A final consideration that is more immediately relevant to psychology is the question about the nature and limitations (or lack thereof) of human consciousness. It is clear that our sense organs have limitations, but it is still unclear whether, and in what ways, consciousness is limited by the evolutionary process. While we may not arrive at anything approaching an answer that achieves consensus, the question should be one that attends us as we explore the issues ahead.

# Chapter 4

## Seeing is Believing and
## Believing is Seeing

We might well say that physical existence is merely an

inference, since we know of matter only in so far as

we perceive psychic images transmitted by the senses.

**C.G. Jung**

*Psychology and Religion*

"*Myxotricha paradoxa* . . . [is a] protozoan, not yet as famous as he should be . . . His cilia are not cilia at all, but individual spirochetes, and at the base of attachment of each spirochete is an oval organelle, embedded in the myxotricha

53

membrane, which is a bacterium. [*Myxotricha paradoxa*] is not an animal after all - it is a company, an assemblage." (Thomas, 1974, p. 145)

The ideas presented in Thomas' book, *Lives of a Cell*, are fascinating and profound, both for the field of biology and for how we view ourselves. Likewise, the discovery many years ago that the single celled Euglena contained characteristics of both plant and animal, brought into question the absoluteness of that distinction. But Thomas' recitation of the structure of *Myxotricha* was only a prelude to his presentation of a more immediately relevant fact.

"Our [human] cilia gave up any independent existence long ago, and our organelles are now truly ours, but the genomes controlling separate parts of our cells are still different genomes, lodged in separate compartments; doctrinally, we are still assemblages." (p. 145-6) " I was raised in the belief that [mitochondria - the cell organelles that arrange for the use of oxygen] were obscure little engines inside my cells, owned and operated by me or my cellular delegates; private, submicroscopic bits of my intelligent flesh. Now, it appears [that they] are total strangers. . . . The DNA of mitochondria is qualitatively different from the DNA of the animal cell

54

nuclei . . . The mitochondria do not arise *de novo* in cells; they are always there, replicating on their own independently of the replication of the cell." (p. 82-3)

Thus, like the physicists, biologists are telling us that things are not exactly as they appear; creatures are not always quite what common sense tells us they are. Our bodies, which most of us have grown up thinking of as virtually synonymous with our "self", actually contain independent bio-machines that control critical functions at the cellular level. If our mitochondria are genetically different from the rest of our bodies, but essential to its function, what does this say about the unity of our self, and its separateness from other selves? Here again, our experience does not fit with the "reality". To say that our experience is therefore an illusion, is not totally accurate either, but it is clear that what we consciously experience is not the ultimate essence of things.

It may be most accurate to say that what we experience is a product of the interaction of the stuff of the universe and the physiological/cultural/linguistic/psychological filters through which we screen and interpret the raw data. While this multi-layered apparatus has evolved in a manner that facilitates our success in our particular environment, it is only one of a virtually infinite number of configurations that could be. Thus, the "reality" we experience, is only one of an infinite number of realities.

While this model is highly complex and there are aspects of it that we do not yet fully comprehend, the general structure is well enough mapped to allow us to carry on a useful discussion. In order to facilitate this discussion, the material has been broken down into two categories:

1. The physiological system - the sense organs and the brain, covered in the present chapter, and

2. The cultural context - the social-linguistic influences which will be addressed in the following chapter.

One of the most important things we know about the sensory system and the brain is that they are not simply passive recorders of environmental stimuli. In the first place, this complex web of cells is a very efficient data reduction system. It keeps us from being overwhelmed by the "blooming, buzzing confusion" of the information with which we are constantly bombarded. Second, it plays a role in organizing the data that is input; generally, but not always, in a fashion that facilitates the survival and functioning of the organism.

The limitations of our sensory organs are well documented. The average human auditory system, for example, responds to sounds in the range of approximately 20 to 20,000 cycles per second. That wave forms outside this range exist is abundantly clear from research with other animals and with mechanical sensing devices. Likewise, the eye is sensitive to an incredibly small segment of the total range of known electromagnetic radiation. While the recognized spectrum of wave lengths ranges from less than one billionth of a meter to more than 1000 meters, the visible spectrum is limited to frequencies between about 400 and 700 billionths of a meter. Our visual sensors simply do not respond to wave lengths outside of this window. Considering the enormous amount of electromagnetic information with which we are constantly assailed, we are fortunate that we are not equipped to perceive more than we do.

It is important to understand that our visual processing system is not better or worse in any ultimate sense, rather, that it has had considerable survival value in our particular ecological niche. Consider for a moment the visual system of the frog. According to the research, frogs respond to only four visual patterns: general outlines, significant movement, sudden decreases in light, and small dark objects moving close to the eye. But it is very ego-centric to conclude that the frog's life is therefore impoverished. The frog is very successfully adapted to its niche, and since it has no knowledge of other visual experiences, we must conclude that it is "happy" with what it has. Like the frog, we are limited in our visual perception, but we can function successfully and be "happy" with what we have been given.

There is a second way in which our sensory organs, in combination with our brain, determine our experience of the world outside. The manner in which our organs of perception function determines not only what data will be permitted entry into awareness, but the form that data will assume and the manner in which it will be organized and interpreted. To further complicate things, it has been found (as some of the following studies show) that our history of experience, as well as structure of the sensory apparatus and the characteristics of the stimuli, plays a role in determining how we experience things.

Over a half a century ago researchers (Ittleson and Kilpatrick, 1951) reported in *Scientific American* the results of a study examining responses to various optical illusions, which showed that what we perceive does not necessarily have an isomorphic correspondence with external events. The authors of the study had subjects sit in a darkened room in which they can see only two points of light which were equidistant from the observer and of equal brightness. When the two lights were near the floor, one about a foot above the other, the upper one was generally perceived as further away than the lower one. If the lights were near the ceiling, the lower one was perceived as the more distant.

A somewhat more complicated experiment utilized two partially inflated balloons, illuminated from a concealed source. The balloons were in fixed positions about one foot apart. Their sizes could be varied by adding or taking away air, and the degree of illumination could be controlled also. When the size of a balloon was increased, it appeared to subjects to move forward; when the size was then decreased it appeared to retreat. Likewise, when the brightness was increased the balloon appeared to move forward, and when decreased it again appeared to retreat.

A second experiment used what is known as the Ames room, a visually distorting room in which the floor slopes upward from left to right, the rear wall recedes from the right

59

to the left, and the windows are of different sizes and trapezoidal in shape. When an observer standing in front of this room looks at it with one eye, the room appears normal - floor level, rear wall perpendicular to the line of sight and windows rectangular and of the same size. The point of these experiments is, of course, to show that perception is never an absolute revelation of what exists "out there".

Another informative study was carried out by researcher Ivo Kohler (1962), utilizing goggles with distorting lenses. Subjects who wore the goggles reported that turning their head from side to side caused objects to become broader, then narrower generating an accordion effect. Moving their heads up and down caused object to slant first one way, then the other. One subject reported that it was as if the world were made of rubber. While, at first, the subjects were disoriented and able to get around only with the greatest difficulty, after several weeks they adapted and were able to function almost normally.

Another goggle experiment in which the lenses transposed the left visual field to the right (and vice versa) and the top to the bottom (and vice versa) left subjects equally disoriented at the outset and equally handicapped in function. However, after several weeks, one of the subjects had so accommodated to the new perceptions that he was able to ride a motorcycle in city traffic.

What is of particular interest here is that individuals whose perceptions are significantly distorted are able, in a relatively short period of time, to adapt to their new "reality", and function almost normally. We may deduce that the visual system is organized in a highly functional fashion, and is capable of great adaptability. In other words, its "purpose" is not to provide our conscious awareness with a point for point accurate picture of some "reality", but rather to provide useful information that can be used in decision making designed to enhance the function of the organism.

This interpretation is reinforced by the reports of the experience of goggle-experiment subjects upon removing their goggles after having become adapted to their goggle-distorted world. Just as they had perceived distortion when they first donned the goggles, these individuals now perceived the "undistorted real world" as distorted in a fashion opposite to the distortion of the goggles.

Another phenomenon which demonstrates how perception can be inconstant is termed figural multistability. The two figures shown in Figure 2 are examples of this. The top drawing is called a Necher cube, after its designer. The figure at the bottom is the reversible goblet first introduced by Edgar Rubin in 1915. Notice that for both drawings, the information received by the retina of he eye and the brain does not change. However, the interpretation of the raw data may change significantly.

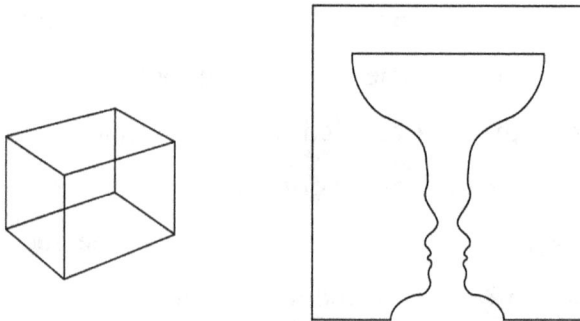

*Figure 2*

Another experiment involving the Ames room (described earlier) produced an additional finding which has been labeled the "Honi phenomenon", after the name of the woman who first manifested it. Typically, when a subject observes a person walk from one side of the illusion-producing Ames room to the other, because of the distorting geometry, the person observed appears to change in size dramatically, growing or shrinking depending on which direction the person walks. Thus, in the typical case study, the observer sticks to his/her assumptions about the shape of the room, even to the extreme of accepting unlikely distortion in the appearance of another person. Honi, however, observing her husband walking from side to side in the Ames room, reported no change in his size, in contrast to her reported perception of a stranger changing size radically under the same conditions.

As subsequent researchers speculated and later confirmed, the Honi phenomenon (and other similar deviations from usual distortions) was attributable, at least in large part, to emotional attachments between the observer and the observed. Honi, and other individuals who had strong emotional connections to persons they observed in distorting conditions, "refused" to see that person distorted, even though strangers were perceived as distorted in the same context. The interested reader can undoubtedly find other examples of these phenomenon; however, those cited above should be sufficient to illustrate the principle.

In commenting on their work and its implications for psychology, Ittleson and Kirkpatrick discussed the prevailing predisposition in scientific circles that there is some perceptual level where there exists absolute objectivity, that is, a one-to-one correspondence between experience and reality. However, Ittleson and Kilpatrick argue that when stimuli or stimulus patterns are treated as though they exist apart from the perceiving organism, it leads to the positing of dichotomies such as organism versus environment and subjective versus objective. They go on to state that the experiments they devised, "arose from a widespread and growing feeling that such dichotomies are false, and that, in practice, it is impossible to leave values and purposes out of consideration in scientific observation. . . . This conclusion, of course, has far-reaching implications for many areas of study, for some assumptions as to what perception is, must underlie any philosophy or comprehensive theory of psychology or science, or even of knowledge in general. Although the particular investigations involved here are restricted to visual perception, this is only a vehicle which carries us into a basic inquiry of much wider significance."

# Chapter 5

## And The Word Was God
## (John 1:1)

We maintain our world with our internal talk. Whenever we finish talking to ourselves, the world is always as it should be. We renew it, we kindle it with life, we uphold it with our internal talk. Not only that, but we also choose our paths as we talk to ourselves. Thus, we repeat the same choices over and over until the day we die because we keep repeating the same internal talk over and over until the day we die.

A warrior is aware that the world will change as soon as he stops talking to himself, and he must be prepared for that monumental jolt.

**Don Juan Matos**

In C. Castaneda, *A Separate Reality*

The role of language in shaping one's experience of the world clearly occupies a central place in the teachings of Yaqui brujo, Don Juan. And while it may be easy for some to discount his philosophy for a variety of reasons, it is not such a simple matter to discount the centuries of thought and writings from those who have practiced Zen meditation, or from the philosopher Wittgenstein, nor the semanticists Korzybski and Whorf. Yet the degree to which language shapes our experience is unrecognized by many, and even when recognized, it is generally not accorded the importance it deserves.

As the material in the previous chapter showed, our experience of our world is, to a significant extent, a creation of our sensory processing apparatus. But the modification of the raw data does not stop with this initial filter. What we

66

ultimately consciously experience is not simply a set of sensory impressions; what we experience is a world of interpreted meaning. There are at least three filters beyond the sensory filter. These include the filters of culture, language and personal experience. The influence of these filters is extremely broad and profound. Ironically, it is this very pervasiveness and depth that cause these filters to remain largely unnoticed.

Among these secondary filters, culture is perhaps the most accessible. Cross cultural contacts often make this influence very apparent. While working with Native Americans in the southwestern United States, anthropologist Alan Dundes came down with a head cold. After observing Dundes blow his nose into his handkerchief, fold it and return it to his pocket, one of the natives asked Dundes if he thought that the stuff from his nose had some special power. Dundes, somewhat bewildered, replied that he didn't. "Then why," the man asked, "do you fold it up in that cloth and save it?" That question would not have been asked by someone born and raised in Madison, Wisconsin. (Dundes, 1964)

More scientific approaches to studying the effects of culture have also yielded some interesting data. Bagby

(1953), using matched Mexican and American subjects, presented them with a series of stereogram slides. The picture seen by one eye was a typical Mexican scene, but the picture seen by the other eye was a typical American scene. The paired scenes were selected to have similar form, texture, light and shadow characteristics. Bagby reported a strong tendency for  Mexican subjects to report seeing only the Mexican scene in each pair, and for American subjects to report seeing only the American scene. He concluded that, "Under conditions of perceptual conflict, as found in the binocular rivalry situation, those figures possessing the more immediate first person meaning predominate."

Cultural differences do not exist only between people of different nations. Bruner and Goodman (1947), for example, explored the cultural differences between different socioeconomic levels within the United States. One of their findings was that children from poorer families tended to see a given coin as larger than their peers from more fortunate families. Bruner's interpretation of this finding was that coins such as these probably had greater day-to-day salience in the lives of those of modest means.

That cultural factors should play a role in determining

values and perceptions is, perhaps, not altogether surprising. However, the extent to which we experience what we are used to experiencing or expect to experience, is greater than one might guess. In one interesting study, Ellson (1941) presented subjects with a paired light and buzzer for many trials. When he unexpectedly presented the light alone, subjects still "heard" the buzzer.

It is important to note here that the scientific community and field of psychology constitute cultures of a sort. Professional training is at least partly a socialization process in which the neophyte professional is indoctrinated with new set of information, methods, ideas and values. The new initiate is indoctrinated with the models of reality deemed accurate, and with the research and analytical methods considered valuable. Polanyi (1958) described this process, pointing out how the established members of an existing profession inculcate new members, and how they reinforce the view of reality implicit in the paradigm of that school, and confirm each other as competent and responsible seekers of knowledge.

Before embarking on our voyage into the primary topic of this chapter, the role of the personal filter should be mentioned at least briefly. This filter is the one most easily comprehended and identifiable to most people. As a result of the Viet Nam war many Americans became aware of Post Traumatic Stress Syndrome and the sometimes dramatic effects it produced in returning veterans. Many people are also aware of how childhood experiences can result in adult preferences or fears. The Japanese film *Rashomon* illustrates beautifully how individual experience is colored by cultural values mediated through personal needs. Similarly, Lawrence Durrell's *Alexandria Quartet* demonstrates how personal point of view shapes one's "reality".

A very compelling analysis of how our filters distort experience at an intrapsychic level is presented in Charles Tart's seminal chapter, *Ordinary Consciousness as a State of Illusion* (Tart, 1975). In the chapter, Tart takes one through a short hypothetical interaction between his subject, Sam, and a stranger, Bill. Tart shows in a millisecond by millisecond analysis how a simple verbal stimulus provokes multiple intrapsychic associations and ensuing feedback loops which so dramatically supplement the stimulus that a simple greeting becomes fraught with implications and meanings (many unconscious), creating an internal melodrama for the subject which is at least as important to him as the perceptual impact of the raw stimulus.

The impact of the personal filter is no less significant than that of other filters, and the fact that it has received a rather cursory examination here should not be taken as evidence of secondary status. Rather, it is the fact that most people are aware of this filter and how it impacts interaction with the environment that has merited it relatively less attention. Therefore, with this albeit brief acknowledgment we return to considering the role of language as a shaper of reality.

Although not identical with it, language is certainly an essential and integral facet of culture. Its influence is pervasive, and according to semanticists, of primary importance in shaping our experience of our world. Benjamin Whorf (1951), for example, wrote, "We cut up and organize the spread and flow of events as we do, largely because, through our mother tongue, we are parties to an agreement to do so, not because nature itself is segmented in exactly that way for all to see." His colleague, Alfred Korzybski (1958), concurred and commented that, "we read unconsciously into the world the structure of the language we use."

Whorf also proposed that, as well as insinuating a

structure, every language precluded certain others. "Every language and every well-knit technical sub-language incorporates certain points of view and certain patterned resistances to widely divergent points of view."

Here, as forcefully as anywhere, one is reminded of the astuteness of Aldous Huxley's (1956) comment on language. "Every individual is at once the beneficiary and victim of the linguistic tradition into which he has been born - the beneficiary inasmuch as language gives access to the accumulated records of other people's experience, the victim insofar as it confirms him in the belief that reduced awareness is the only awareness, and as it bedevils his sense of reality, so that he is all too apt to take his concepts for data, and his words for actual things." ( p. 23-24.)

To try to identify all the respects in which language imposes a structure on our perceptions is certainly a challenging task - much like asking a fish to discuss how the qualities of water affect her experience in, and perception of, the world. And, since we must use the language we are attempting to examine as a tool in the examination, the task is doubly difficult.

According to the experts, it is through the comparison of

our own language with other languages that we can achieve the best understanding of the reality shaping characteristics of each. "Languages differ not only in how they build their sentences, but in how they break down nature to secure the elements to put in those sentences. . . . Thus, English and similar tongues lead us to think of the universe as a collection of rather distinct objects and events corresponding to words. Indeed, this is the implicit picture of classical physics and astronomy - that the universe is essentially a collection of detached objects of different sizes." (Klein, 1956-57, p. 93)

According to semanticists, other languages organize reality differently. The Hopi language, for example, classifies events by duration. Events of short duration, e.g., flame, wave, puff, can only be verbs. Only events of longer duration may be nouns. The treatment of time is also different in such a way that the Hopi language is reputed to be a much better vehicle for discussing the notion of Einstein's relative time than is English.

And, according to anthropologist Dorothy Lee (1950), the Trobriand Islanders communicate in a non-linear, present-centered fashion that lacks any dynamic relating of acts. Trobriand speech patterns are therefore jerky to our ears and given in points rather than connecting lines.

Based on the information acquired by the semanticists, we might speculate that one reason that we in Western society, despite our proximity to those who have created the new physics, have remained unaware of these ideas, is the difficulty of explaining them in English. Attempts to explicate these concepts in our mother tongue result in statements that sound paradoxical at best, and more often as patent nonsense. Take, for example, the comment by Robert Oppenheimer. "If we ask, for instance, whether the position of an electron remains the same, we must say no; if we ask whether the electron's position changes with time we must also say no; if we ask whether the electron is at rest, we must say no; if we ask whether it is in motion we must say no." (Capra, 1975, p. 154)

To repeat the earlier cited words of de Broglie, "Each observer, as his time passes, discovers, so to speak, new slices of space-time which appear to him as successive aspects of the material world, though in reality the ensemble of events constituting space-time exist prior to his knowledge of them." (Capra, p.185) Fritjof Capra advises us that, "The distinction between matter and empty space finally had to be abandoned when it became evident that virtual particles can come into being spontaneously out of the void and vanish again into the void." (Capra, p. 222)

Some physicists have, of course, recognized the linguistic problem. Niels Bohr (1987), in one of his fine essays noted that, "all our ordinary verbal expressions bear the stamp of our customary forms of perception, from the point of view of which the existence of quantum action is an irrationality." (p. 19) Sir Edmund Whittaker once regretted the use of the term 'curvature of space'. "It is an unfortunate custom," he said, "because curvature, in the sense of bending, is a meaningless term except when the space is immersed in another space, whereas the property of being non-Euclidean is an intrinsic property which has nothing to do with such immersion. However, nothing can be done but to utter a warning that what mathematicians understand by the term curvature is not what the word connotes in ordinary speech: . . . Curvature has nothing to do with the shape of space." (Clark, 1971, p. 203)

One observant acquaintance of mine has even noted that the geometry of our assumptive physical space has spilled over into the virtual space of our personal and intellectual relationships. He has suggested that, in an important sense, *plain* sense is really *plane* sense. We also talk, for example, of having a *position* on an issue, of having a *point* of view, or of being *close* to someone. One might say that he is *leaning* in this or that direction, of that he is *inclined* to believe something. In this sense, our linguistic patterns have superimposed a quasi-physical structure on a conceptual space where there is no physical dimensional structure.

Whether the concepts that physicists are trying to express are inherently difficult for us to understand, most of us will probably never know, because it is only through language, which is obviously lacking in this case, that most of us will ever be exposed to them. Under the current linguistic circumstances, the ideas noted above contain contradictions of such a fundamental nature that they cannot be understood without recourse to some sort of consideration beyond the scope of language.

Not that the problem is confined to modern physics. Semanticists have admonished us to remember in all our linguistic enterprises that the word is not the thing. A word is nothing more than an abstraction - an arbitrary and conventionalized symbol. Cassirer (1944, p. 109) reminds us that, "Language is, by its very nature and essence, metaphorical." This is not to say that all words are actually metaphors. All words are symbols, or, as some would say, a map. And semanticists are quick to warn us that the map is not the territory. Some words which have simple concrete referents - shoe, tree, cup, dog - have a low level of ambiguity and generally cause little disagreement or confusion. Other words - spirituality, communism, love, self - are more abstract and may be interpreted quite differently by different persons.

Reflecting on the origins of this arbitrary and conventionalized system of communication, Korzybski notes, "every language . . . reflects in its own structure that of the world assumed by those who evolved the language." (in Klein, 1956-57, p. 91) Thus, if the assumptions of our predecessors were incorrect or incomplete, then, to the extent that we fail to recognize the limitations and inaccuracies of our language, and make appropriate corrections, we are caught in a fiendishly clever linguistic trap.

Ludwig Wittgenstein (1953), a man of no small repute in the field of linguistic analysis, has told us that, "Philosophy is a battle against the bewitchment of our intelligence by means of language. My aim is to teach you to pass from a place of disguised nonsense to something that is patent nonsense. He who understands me finally recognizes [my propositions] as senseless."

Norman O. Brown (1959), discussing the psychoanalytic analysis of language and the poets, suggests, "if language is essentially a neurotic compromise between the erotic (pleasure) and the operational (reality) principles, it follows that consciousness, in the artistic use of the language, is subversive to its own instrument and seeks to pass beyond it . . . The goal [of the artistic use of language] is an experience essentially ineffable." (p. 73) Brown might well have added that, at times, the goal of scientific language is also ultimately an experience essentially ineffable.

Although we have so far considered contemporary thinkers, the attempt to deal with the bewitchment of intelligence by means of language goes back thousands of years. Traditions that predated the Buddha have descendants in early Zen writings and practice. Sheldon Klein (1956-57), in his thoughtful paper on Zen notes that, "the early Zen sutras contained a formal system of general semantics directly comparable to twentieth century Western systems. . . . [and] the later koan discipline (after the eleventh century, A.D.) is a method for acquiring an intuitive grasp of semantics." ( p.

88)

Not only did the Zen masters recognize the problem inherent in language, they instituted an antidote. This antidote became an essential aspect of the Zen life style, a practice becoming more and more familiar in the West. Specifically, two practices are aimed at helping the Zen student break out of the chains of language. These are the Zen koan and the practice of Zen meditation.

The koans are rationally/linguistically insoluble verbal problems given to the student to "solve". Perhaps the most familiar example of a koan is, "What is the sound of one hand clapping?" If the master's ploy is successful, the student will experience a breakthrough in which he sees the paradox, and recognizes that the solution lies outside the structure of language. Klein, following Bridgman, proposes that we in the West also have koans - namely the problems posed by modern physics, an idea which is echoed in Capra's work.

The second of the antidotes, the practice of Zen meditation, is an exercise in non-verbal, non-evaluative awareness. The novice learns by sitting quietly but with fierce attention, and allowing the flora and fauna of his mind (Don Juan's internal talk) to run through their cycles until they gradually lose their momentum and he/she achieves a clear, thoughtless state of focused awareness. Where the koans force a direct struggle with the chains of language and rationality, meditation attempts to overcome the products of the "monkey mind" through a more passive attention and acceptance without attachment.

At the conclusion of his discourse, Klein makes an interesting observation. Despite the fact that he has stressed the similarities of Zen semantics and Western semantics, he proposes that the respective purposes for which the principles are employed are quite different. The general semantics of the West, he suggests, were developed to manipulate the world of abstraction with greater precision, that is, to minimize the confusion that arises through the use of language. The goal of Zen, on the other hand, is to facilitate the complete abandonment of the inaccuracies and illusions created by the non-conscious use of language.

If we accept it as accurate, Klein's point is an extremely salient one for psychology, for it is the discipline most appropriate to carry this line of thinking to its logical (or should we say illogical) conclusion. Given the quantity and quality of material indicating that the world we experience is a limited and filtered version of what exists "out there", not to mention the lofty status of its sources, it is time that we take this idea seriously and take steps to make sure that it is thoughtfully explored, particularly in the field of psychology.

# Prologue
# to the Last Four Chapters

This volume is made up of two distinct parts. The first five chapters are focused on providing the empirical basis for establishing the context from which to evaluate our current state. Given that the basic work in this area had already been done, this involved selecting appropriate material and organizing it into a meaningful and understandable pattern.

The second section, Chapters 6, 7, 8, and 9, involves a different and more analytical, yet to some extent creative, endeavor. It is an attempt to assess the strengths and limitations of our current situation and to formulate ideas about what directions are most likely to produce useful avenues for study. Thus, to a certain degree, this is more open to conjecture than the first five chapters, and should therefore be considered as the opening round of a discussion about the possible future direction(s) of Western Psychology.

Chapter 6 is focused on the strengths and contributions, but also the limitations, of Western Psychology. Chapter 7 is an attempt to identify the elements of ancient Eastern Psychology, that is, the psychology that is found primarily, but not exclusively, in ancient Buddhist texts, and to articulate these elements in such a way as to render them more consistent with, and understandable within, the conceptual proclivities of the West. Chapter 8 is an endeavor to sketch a new frame of reference for future psychology which incorporates both Western and Eastern Psychologies integrated through the prism of modern physics, and informed by lessons of the study of perception, language, culture and personality. The final chapter is an exploration of the implications of adopting a new frame of reference in the study of human psychology.

# Chapter 6

## Modern Psychology:
## The Objectivity-Subjectivity Dilemma

A man saw Nasrudin searching for something
on the ground.
"What have you lost, Mullah?" he asked.
"My key," Nasrudin replied.
So the man dropped to his knees
and they both looked together.
After a period of fruitless search the man asked,
"Where exactly did you drop it?"
"In front of my house," Nasrudin answered.
"Then why are you looking here?" the puzzled man queried.
"There is more light here than in front of my house."

**Sufi Parable**

The first step in evaluating any entity or discipline is considering its strengths and weaknesses. Modern psychology as it exists in America is a thriving enterprise. Every major university has a psychology or behavioral science department, there is ongoing psychological research of many varieties, and there are millions of psychotherapists working with a wide array of clients all across the country. Awareness of, and the development of treatments for, various types of psychopathology is the result of dedicated study by countless mental health professionals. It would be absurd to propose that all of this is of no value. In fact, research has shown that psychotherapy is an effective tool for many. And it would be hard to argue that education about the role and importance of psychology in overall health is not beneficial. Thus, the present chapter is not an attempt to paint all of modern psychology as misguided or useless. Rather, the goal is to try to identify the areas in which it is successful, and to also identify its limitations.

Let us first consider those areas in which modern psychology has been beneficial. We can point to areas like neuropsychology and the study of perception, developmental psychology, learning and conditioning, intelligence and personality testing, the study of psychopathology, social psychology, and the field of psychotherapy as providing material that has been both informative and useful. We have already seen how the study of perception has provided important information. And it would be hard to deny that the refinement of our ability to delineate and identify different types of psychopathology and provide differential treatments for them is a good thing. And, more generally, the growing awareness of psychological factors as important in overall health is undeniably a step in the right direction.

Given that modern psychology has made significant contributions, do we really need to initiate a critique? While many in the field might disagree, I believe that, given the knowledge we have from physics, from studies of perception, from linguists, from philosophy of science, and the assessments provided by psychologists such as Sigmund Koch, the time is ripe for a re-evaluation of the goals, philosophical framework and methods of modern psychology. This is particularly true, and increasingly pressing, since we have an imposing alternative in the ancient psychology of the East. The reader is encouraged to avoid framing this discussion in an either-or manner, and to recall instead that page from the volume of modern physics which delineates the theory of complementarity regarding the nature of light.

The emphasis in modern psychology during the past hundred or so years has been on the scientific method. The adoption of the objectivist scientific approach (evident in the behaviorist movement), and the adoption of logical positivism and operationism, brought to a head the attempt in Hume's work to find a way to obviate individual, subjective, fallible human experience. It is not difficult to understand why this approach rapidly gained favor, nor should we deny that it should still have a significant role in generating data that leads to understandings about humans. Like other experiments, however, we need to consider both the process and the results in a straightforward and unbiased manner using the most appropriate available frame of reference.

In the first place, we must consider the goals and objectives of modern psychology. If, as Koch has surmised, psychology's method was chosen before its subject matter was selected, then we need to review and consider carefully our choice of subject matter and goals. And ask ourselves, are these goals clear, meaningful and comprehensive when observed within a post-Einsteinian, subjectivist, framework?

Second, we need to look at the methods utilized by modern psychology, and ask to what extent are these methods appropriate and sufficient for reaching our stated goals. Do they need to be modified and/or complemented by the inclusion of other methods?

Third, we must ask how the theoretical basis fits with the current knowledge about the nature of "reality".

Therefore, let us consider in this context what the findings of modern physics mean for our assessment of modern psychology. The notion that psychological research should be objective and empirical runs strong and deep in the modern mainstream tradition. Students of psychology are taught that there are psychological facts that can be discovered in an unbiased fashion by rigorously applying the appropriate tools. Now while some psychologists may recognize that their system is not entirely objective, the overall behavior of the field supports the current ideology.

Physicists, on the other hand, have argued that complete objectivity is impossible. The universe, they assert, is governed by laws of relativity and quantum mechanics, and any time we try to study it, we determine in a significant way what we will find by the concepts we use, the way we measure them, and the manner in which our experiments are designed.

What psychologists have done in designing an "objective" research strategy is to reduce the effects of certain kinds of individual bias. In general, this has been accomplished by setting up studies in such a fashion that, regardless of who collects or analyzes the data, the results will be the same (assuming appropriate training of all researchers). Part and parcel of this strategy has been a proclivity for quantification and operational definition.

While this has been an interesting and, in certain respects, successful venture on the part of psychologists, it contains some serious flaws. Even a cursory consideration of the bases of scientific psychology will demonstrate this to be true. The operational definition, a point at which physics and psychology have an interface, is a good place to begin. Percy Bridgeman's operationism (of which the operational definition is a descendant) was an important contribution to the development of modern physics. But as Marx and Hillix (1963) point out, "It is probably fair to say that operationism is incomplete, is beset with philosophical difficulties, and, if taken literally, cannot provide an altogether consistent program for scientific advance." (p.15)

Yet, psychologists borrowed from Bridgeman in hopes that they could resolve certain problems of their own. In it simplest form, this doctrine proposes that a concept can best be defined (in fact, is synonymous with) the operations that are involved in measuring it. Thus we get the famous (or infamous) statement from a noted psychologist that "intelligence is what intelligence tests measure". Operationism does solve the problem of the definition of a concept, but not without raising the equally serious problem of meaningfulness or ultimate validity.

The controversy over intelligence testing provides graphic illustration of the problem. Psychologists have proposed, and shown, that the totality (or even the most important aspects) of an individual's ability is not necessarily reflected in their IQ score. It should not be surprising that a test, originally designed to predict success in the French school system, developed by those with white, middle class experiences and values, is limited and biased. The IQ test obviously measures something, and something that has value in certain circumstances, but whether it is the most important "mental" ability (as some seem to believe) is another question entirely.

Many strategies and procedures have been developed as ways of validating psychological tests. Among them are some very clever and thoughtful approaches. Construct validation, factor analysis, the Campbell-Fiske multitrait-multimethod matrix (Campbell & Fiske, 1959), and known groups validation have all been invoked as strategies in demonstrating that a given test really measures what it claims to measure. Nonetheless, there are no empirical criteria which exist "out there" against which to evaluate the verisimilitude of our measures. Thus, we are left with what ultimately turn out to be a whole host of subjective decisions on the way to validating a measure of a psychological construct.

For example, the development of a psychological measure might proceed something like this: 1.) conceptualize the construct to be measured - necessarily a subjective and creative grouping and/or ordering of experience; 2.) make up items to be included in the measure - another subjective process including choosing the content, wording, format and number of items; 3.) select the items for the final form of the measure - largely an empirical endeavor, but still one based on a theoretical position which cannot be empirically verified;

4.) validate the measure - this typically employs statistical analyses, but the criteria are subjective, and the measures against which any given measure is validated have the same subjective origin.

Thus, the defining and measuring of psychological constructs has a large subjective component. The concepts and constructs of psychology do not exist "out there" waiting to be discovered. They exist only as we make them up and elaborate them. They may, indeed, have practical utility, but they remain our creations, and there is no ultimate standard against which to validate them. This creative process is inevitably affected by our personal, cultural, and linguistic biases. Behavioral psychology escapes from complete subjectivity, but only in a relatively small section of the larger study of human psychology.

The question of whether psychology (or any other area of study for that matter) can be completely objective has been clearly and resoundingly answered in the negative. Percy Bridgeman (1927), the father of Operationism, concluded that, "in the last analysis, science is only my private science." Psychologist Michael Wertheimer (1972) echoed the same sentiment when he opined, "Yet it seems impossible to refute the epistemological logic leading to a fundamentally solipsistic view of the nature of all human knowledge, whether in psychology or in any of the other disciplines and sciences. In some ultimate sense, you cannot transcend subjective experience." (p. 128)

That this is an unpalatable, if not totally inadmissible, proposition for many involved in psychology is quite clear. But, as Marx and Hillix (1963) so adroitly ask, "If reality is but an ambiguous figure, and what we see in it is determined by the paradigm we have already accepted, then what happens to the foundations of science?" (p. 21) Those psychological researchers who rely on a philosophy of science grounded in an objectivistic analysis of the scientific enterprise will not accept this neo-solipsism without a struggle.

Even the rational-logical objectivist systems are apparently not safe from disruption, however. Psychologist Ken Pelletier (1977) informs us that, "Kurt Godel [provides a] formal mathematical demonstration of a non-logical, non-objective component of bias in all logical paradigms. This work of fundamental logic is known as Godel's theorem. . . . Godel demonstrates the incompleteness of logic by strictly formal methods, and proves that there must exist in logic, a proposition that says that it is not a proposition. This proof has not been refuted, and stands as a testimony that the hope of logicians to logicize mathematics and other sciences is ill-founded. . . . In demonstrating the irrational aspect of the proposition that denies itself, Godel presents a formal proof of the irrational component in all logical systems and undermines the internal coherence of logic as a closed system."

The resistance of many to accepting a subjectivist point of view, though great, may not be insurmountable. Michael Wertheimer's (1972) comments on his own struggle with the problem are enlightening. "Some may feel that such a philosophy of convincingness is a philosophy of defeat, of pessimism, perhaps even of nihilism. I must confess that when I first started thinking about these issues, I was still grasping for the straw of absolutism, and this position struck me the same way; I struggled to avoid the solipsistic box into which logic seemed to stuff me. But I think that the quest for, and insistence upon, absolutes over and beyond one's own experience is at best an unnecessary crutch, or, at worst, a set of goggles that blind or distort rather than correct. Why despair just because it is ultimately impossible to transcend individual cognition?  Why need one try to prove or assume the existence of a reality independent of experience?"  ( p. 122)

But is there even really a conflict here?  The subjective-objective issue has long been a central one for science.  We are taught to think of this as a dichotomous variable.  By linguistic convention we situate subjectivity and objectivity as mutually exclusive opposites.  When we look behind the language filter, however, we see that the problem disappears.  All experience is subjective, and there are no opposites or exceptions.  When we talk of objectivity in research we simply mean that we have employed certain types of methodological controls in our experiments to reduce the number of variables we must take into consideration, and thus reduce the potential sources of error or bias in our results.  Sampling procedures are one example of a procedure designed to reduce unwanted error.  (Some of these procedures can raise the question of generalizability, but we will ignore this issue for the time being.)

Thus, objectivity is not the opposite of subjectivity, it is simply a special subset of it.  There is no dichotomous dimension, no conflict.  Just a linguistic illusion.  To be fair and accurate, the "objective" scientific approach has proved useful in solving certain kinds of problems, thereby conferring on humankind a power to control and manipulate various aspects of the environment. Many of these have proved valuable in making life safer and more comfortable. But, it is also the case that many of the results of scientific endeavors are proving to have very negative consequences for humans and for the planet. Thus, objectivity is neither good or bad in and of itself. It is simply a special case of subjectivity that may be used to achieve certain ends.

There is another condition of science and of scientific psychology which is generally conceived of as implicit in the idea of objectivity. That condition is that data to be analyzed must be public, that is, that it must be derived from events that we all can see (or theoretically are observable by anyone) and that the relevant values obtained from any experiment are quantified and written down in a conventional format. The assumption is that by making the data a quantified public event, the results can be reviewed and verified (or discounted) by anyone with proper training. Intra-individual (subjective) experience is viewed as more subject to the effects of personal bias and the distortions that cannot be identified by public consensus.

That this situation should obtain in the current culture of Western Psychology is not surprising. But it is important that we recognize that making data that has inherently subjective underpinnings public does not confer on it greater ultimate validity or meaningfulness. The fact that it conforms to the rules borrowed from other sciences concerned with other aspects of nature hardly makes it the *sine qua non* for the study of human psychology. As history has shown, group consensus can be just as wrong (sometime far more wrong) than individual opinion.

If Western scientists are devoted to the ideas of objectivity and empiricism as essential components of method, they are no less committed to the idea of cause and effect as a description of events in the universe. Psychologists are part of this tradition. Because this concept is so deeply ingrained, and because it has proven itself useful in many practical affairs, it is doubtful that most will ever give it up. Yet it is important to note that the concept of causality has never had unquestioned status in modern Western philosophy. Hume pointed out that the repeated concomitance of events is not sufficient data on which to base a judgment of causation. Our belief in the principle of causality, according to Hume, may well be no more that a kind of illusion of the indoctrinated consciousness. Despite the fact that no one has successfully repudiated Hume's argument, the belief in causality has been bedrock in Western science.

However, this fundament of science was shaken by the findings of physicists studying subatomic phenomena. As noted earlier, at the subatomic level, the principle of causality lost its claim to universal applicability. Particle waves appear and disappear in apparently random profusion. Radiation is emitted by radioactive elements without identifiable cause. And, although Einstein ever refused to believe that God played dice with the universe, most high energy physicists have agreed that, at the very least, the concept of causality cannot be meaningfully applied to many of the phenomena they study.

Even in the "middle range" of natural phenomena, where the concept has a strong basis in common sense and observed associations, and has enjoyed an almost universal acceptance, certain problems are evident. As Morison (1960) shows so nicely in his brief history of the causes of malaria, what is identified as "the cause" depends upon the contemporary state of knowledge, frame of reference, and investigatory tools.

This theme was subsequently elaborated on by Plutchik (1968). "Whatever the reason, medical men have found it congenial to assume that they could find something called "the cause" of a particular disease. In general, the procedure has been to select as "the cause" that element in the situation which one could do the most about. Thus, in ancient and medieval times, malaria, as its name implies, was thought to be due to the bad air of the lowlands. As a result, towns were built on the tops of hills, as one notices in much of Italy today.

"At this stage it seemed reasonable enough to regard bad air as the cause of malaria, but soon the introduction of quinine to Europe from South America suggested another approach. Apparently quinine acted on some situation within the patient to relieve and often cure him completely. Toward the end of the [nineteenth century] the malarial parasite was discovered in the blood of patients suffering from the disease. The effectiveness of quinine was explained by its ability to eliminate this parasite from the blood. The parasite now became "the cause", and those who could afford the cost of quinine, and were reasonably regular in their habits were enabled to escape the most serious ravages of the disease. It did not disappear as a public health problem, however; and further study was given to the chain of causality. These studies were shortly rewarded by the discovery that the parasite was transmitted by certain species of mosquitoes. For practical purposes "the cause" of epidemic malaria became the mosquito, and attention was directed to control its activities.

"Observations such as this point to the probability that epidemic malaria is the result of a nicely balanced set of social and economic, as well as biological factors, each of which has to be present at the appropriate level. We are still completely unable to describe these sufficient conditions with any degree of accuracy, but we know what to do in an epidemic area because we have focused attention on three or four of the most necessary ones."

When we look at the equally complex situation of human experience and behavior, the attempt to specify causes is equally problematic. (The attempt to avoid the difficulty by employing the term antecedent conditions, is a step in the right direction, but doesn't really solve the problem.) To think that we can routinely and easily specify all the significant elements leading up to the appearance of a particular phenomenon is a problematic proposition for many reasons, and we should view it cautiously. This does not mean, however, that we can never identify correlations between events and invent solutions that have practical consequences. It is crucial, however, that we be able to identify the conditions under which this principle applies, and the limitations of such exercises.

Even within the parameters where the idea of causality is useful, there is the potential for difficulty. Because of the way in which socio-cultural factors have shaped our way of defining the world, we arrange and name it in certain ways, and, therefore, assign causality in certain ways and to certain types of elements. Someone from a different culture and tradition might construct the elements of the world using a very different format, yet still obtain practical results. Studies of different approaches to healing (e.g., Western Medicine vs. traditional Chinese Medicine) suggest that, despite different ideas about the construction and operation of the body and widely divergent terms, each is capable of positing causal relations that lead to "cures" of various physical health problems.

The difficulty in using the concept of causality in human affairs is pointed out by the wise fool of the Sufi literature, Nasrudin:

*"What is fate?' Nasrudin is asked by a scholar.*

*"An endless succession of intertwined events, each influencing the other." Nasrudin replies.*

*"That is hardly a satisfactory answer," the scholar counters. "I believe in cause and effect."*

*"Very well," rejoins the Mullah, "Look at that." He points at a procession passing in the street. "That man is being taken to be hanged. Is that because someone gave him a silver piece and enabled him to buy the knife with which he committed the murder; or is it because someone saw him do it; or because nobody stopped him?"*

To anyone familiar with these problems it is clear that the foundations of the science of psychology are not as secure as many would like to think. But it is of equal importance to consider the kinds of progress (or lack thereof) that the science of psychology has made during its tenure. One of the most qualified to comment on this is Sigmund Koch, the appointee of the American Psychological Association to plan and direct a comprehensive study of the current status of psychology.  Koch (1969) reported:

"The idea that psychology - like the natural sciences on which it is modeled - is a cumulative or progressive discipline is simply not born out by its history.  Indeed, the hard knowledge gained by one generation typically disenfranchises the theoretical fictions of the last.  Psychology's larger generalizations are not specified and refined over time and effort.  They are merely replaced.  Throughout psychology's history as a 'science', the hard knowledge it has deposited has been uniformly negative. . . . After all this scientific effort our actual insight into the learning process - reflected in every humanly important context to which learning is relevant - has not improved one jot. . . .

"Biological psychology is perhaps the one area in which some approximation of the analytic pattern of science can be fruitfully applied.  The 100 year history of 'scientific psychology' has proved that most other domains that psychologists have sought to order in the name of science, and through simulations of the analytical pattern definitive of science, simply do not and can not meet the conditions for meaningful application of this analytical pattern.

"When I say that designation as 'science' only vitiates and

104

distorts many legitimate and important domains of psychological study, it is well to understand what I am not saying. I am not saying that psychological studies should not be empirical, should not strive towards the rational classification of observed events, should not essay shrewd, tough-minded and differentiated analyses of the interdependences among significant events. I am not saying that statistical and mathematical methods are inapplicable everywhere. I am not saying that no sub-fields of psychology can be regarded as parts of science.

"I am saying that in many fields close to the heart of the psychological studies, such concepts as 'law', 'experiment', 'measurement', 'variable', 'control', and 'theory' do not behave as their homonyms do in the established sciences. Thus, the term 'science' cannot be properly applied to perception, cognition, motivation, learning, social psychology, psychopathology, personology, esthetics, the study of creativity, or the empirical study of phenomena relevant to the domain of the extant humanities. To persist in applying this highly charged  metaphor is to shackle these fields with highly unrealistic expectations; the inevitable heuristic effect is the enaction of imitation science." (p. 66-7)

One might compare the situation of psychology to that of Nasrudin in the parable related at the beginning of the chapter. Because the methods of science provided meaningful and useful results in their disciplines they were adopted by psychologists in an attempt to bring research power and respectability to the fledgling field. However, as Koch has pointed out, the subject matter was imposed upon the methods rather than vice versa - a Procrustean solution to the problem of deciding what was appropriate to study. And, as Marx and Hillix (1963) note, "Failure to attack problems because they do not fit into a fixed methodological framework is always dangerous in science. Only the most basic and general premises of science . . . are sufficiently well established to accept even tentatively." (p. 160) While searching in the light of the scientific method has been easier in many respects, e.g., gaining general acceptance and obtaining grant money, it now appears that it may be very difficult to find the key to understanding human consciousness by searching only in this light.

# Chapter 7

## Ancient Psychology

Understanding my teachings in the wrong way
is like a man trying to catch a poisonous snake
by grabbing it with his hand, and getting bitten.
If you do not practice the Dharma correctly,
you may come to understand it as the opposite
of what was intended.

**Sutra on Knowing a Better Way to Catch a Snake**

The faculty of voluntarily bringing back
a wandering attention, over and over again,
is the very root of judgment, character and will.

**William James**

In contrast to modern psychology, ancient psychology has roots that can be traced back at least as far as 1500 B.C. The most well-developed of the Eastern traditions is found in the Buddhist literature, and it is this material that will be considered. What becomes clear to anyone who spends time studying this literature is that, although it is written using concepts and equations that seem paradoxical, or even opaque, they also embody an extensive and well-articulated system of psychology. It is these psychological formulations that will be the primary subject of this chapter.

An issue that needs to be addressed at the outset of our discussion of Eastern Psychology is the general conceptions that it is a religion and is characterized by mysticism and spirituality. In looking at the core principles one soon recognizes that nothing could be farther from the truth. Without question Eastern Psychology recognizes and accepts non-ordinary states of reality. But electroencephalographic (EEG) research has clearly demonstrated that these experiences are no more than the correlates of various states of brain wave activity, (see, for example, Horan, 2009) that can be achieved through concerted meditative practice. While access to these states may, to some degree, be predicated on genetic predispositions, this is no different that other human endeavors such as sports, science or art. Interestingly, the work of Horan and others (e.g., Gabora, 2010, who explores the implications of brain cell assembly architecture) suggests strongly that the deeper meditative states - via their interaction with memory - are, in fact, the basis of creativity. Although the experiences of those who achieve deep meditative states my be unfamiliar to most of us, they are, theoretically at least, available to everyone. Labeling them mystical, spiritual or magical is not only inaccurate and ignorant, it exemplifies the kind of linguistic duplicity that prevents/inhibits the kind of study that will lead to progress in understanding our nature and our capacities.

The first passage quoted at the top of this chapter was included for a very specific reason. The Buddha realized that it is quite possible to misinterpret his teachings and go far astray from the message he intended to convey. (This is equally true for students of science.) He also recognized that people can become attached to the words and/or concepts presented in teachings. That was why he admonished his followers that all teachings were like a raft - that is, they are only a vehicle to be used in the search for understanding, not an end in themselves. This metaphor was necessary because of the tendency of many people to mistake rigid adherence to teachings or rules as an end in themselves. And so we must recognize that Buddhist practices are only a means to an end. One might consider whether or not it is useful to apply the same standard to the practices and methods of science.

In considering ancient psychology we should use the same criteria as those employed in evaluating modern psychology. To review:

1. Are the goals clear, meaningful and comprehensive in a Post-Einsteinian, subjectivist, framework?

2. Are the methods appropriate and effective?

3. Does the theoretical basis fit with the current state of knowledge about "reality"?

Because much of the work in the last area has already been done, let us start with criteria number three. Fritjof Capra (1975), in *The Tao of Physics*, presents the findings of modern physics regarding the nature of the physical world and compares them with the teachings of Eastern thought. It should be remembered that Eastern thought is presented in translation, both from a different language and culture, as well as from a distant time. The language is metaphorical and the logic paradoxical. While this makes for difficult reading when considered alone, when compared with the findings of modern physics, much of the mystery disappears. The phrase, "emptiness is form, and form is emptiness", seems nonsensical when viewed from the perspective of one apprehending a Newtonian billiard ball world through the five senses. However, when we consider it through the lens of modern physics, which tells us that matter and energy are indistinguishable, and that all that appears solid to the senses is actually mostly space, the statement equating form and emptiness makes perfect sense. The ancient notions of interdependent origination and interpenetration of material forms are also quickly confirmed when we consider, through the eyes of the physicist, a universe of flowing energy/matter. The concepts of Samsara (the world of illusion) and Nirvana, (the ineffable reality behind it), are also ratified by modern physics. It is quite clear that the ancient sages had an avenue to understanding that rivals modern science.

Regarding criteria number one, the goal of Buddhist practice is no less than a clear understanding of the nature of the world free from perceptual and conceptual distortions. Not so much from an understanding of the theoretical/mathematical formulations of subatomic or cosmic physics, but rather a direct experience of life free from avoidable distortions. The purpose of setting such a goal is not to become the possessor of a piece of "scientific" knowledge, but rather to achieve release from the delusion imposed by conditioning and ignorance and thereby pass beyond conventional Western notions of knowledge to a more universal definition. While science uses a different method, and tends to focus on intermediate objectives in the physical world (to give us power over our environment in order to make our lives less difficult, uncomfortable and dangerous) the ultimate goal is much the same, to reduce ignorance/delusion, and, hence, suffering.

Regarding criteria two, we may say that the method of Buddhist practice varies significantly from that of modern Western science. Students of Buddhism study consciousness through conscious awareness. Many Western psychologists consider this method of study "soft" in contrast to Western empiricism. In fact, in the truest sense of the word, serious practitioners of Zen meditation, who scrupulously attend to all experience in a completely non-evaluative fashion, may be the most radical empiricists around. As history has shown, the result of a long term commitment to this practice results in an experience and point of view that is consistent across practitioners and across time. Thus, there is a very "public" aspect attesting to the reliability of the discoveries of meditators. And, if one recalls the lessons of modern physics regarding the subjective-objective dimension, and the illusions created by perception, language, culture and belief systems, then the practice of meditation makes as much sense as a method of study of human psychology as does statistical analysis. Further, as we shall see, Buddhist teachings are actually an extremely well-articulated system of psychology. (The terms Buddhist Psychology and Eastern Psychology are used interchangeably in what follows.)

It is worth noting that the main method of study utilized by Eastern Psychology, i.e., meditation, has been quite extensively studied by modern Western scientists. As Walsh and Shapiro (2006) point out, there have been hundreds of studies of meditation-responsive variables including psychological, physiological and bio-chemical parameters. Research has shown meditation effective in relieving stress-related disorders, in ameliorating hormonal disorders such as type 2 diabetes, in enhancing immune function in cancer

113

patients, and in decreasing pain in multiple chronic pain syndromes. It has been successfully used in the treatment of anxiety, hypertension, insomnia, panic and phobic disorders, and substance abuse. Walsh and Shapiro also report that mindfulness meditation appears to enhance concentration, learning ability, academic performance and has been shown effective on some measures of creativity.

But what of the structure and content of Eastern Psychology. One can find extensive expositions of this psychology in the *Abhidharma,* or in discussions of this material (e.g., Thera, 1998, and Brazier, 1995). A complete discourse on Buddhist psychology is beyond the scope or intent of this volume; rather, that which follows is a condensed version of this material - some might call it the highlights - drawn from Brazier, Thera and various works of Thich Nhat Hanh, primarily, *The Heart of the Buddha's Teachings*.

What we have come to identify as Buddhist Psychology has its roots in earlier Eastern traditions, but elaborates substantially on its predecessors. Being a product of its time and culture, it is distinctly different from modern Western Psychology, but there are areas where the overlap is quite remarkable. Introspectionism, an early entrant in modern psychology, appeared for a brief moment at the beginning of the 20th century, as did the thinking of American psychologist, William James (whose surprising quote is recorded at the beginning of this chapter), but these were eclipsed by behaviorism, as psychologists attempted to gain credibility by adopting the kinds of methodology that had propelled physics into the forefront of modern attention. Decades later, cognitive psychology and learning theory covered some of the same ground first considered millennia earlier and half a world away. Subsequently, meditation and mindfulness, mainstays of the Buddhist tradition, became areas of interest which influenced various Western therapeutic approaches.

Yet Buddhist Psychology has a flavor all its own, based on a different, but no less rigorous, set of premises. A psychological basis was essential to Buddhism because, unlike Christianity or Islam which prescribe a belief system that adherents are required to adopt on the basis of faith, Buddhism laid out a set of practices, based on a careful study of how the human mind works, for achieving release from human suffering. More specifically, Buddhist Psychology describes how the senses and concepts/belief systems filter and distort "reality", and how the untrained mind can generate inaccurate thoughts which can, in turn, create excessive and distracting emotions. These often lead to unwarranted conclusions which can result in destructive and self-destructive actions. The goal of Buddhist practice is to achieve, through rigorous self-observation, the ability to see past the world of appearances and one's mental creations, and to experience the mind/world as it is, undistorted by our linguistic and conceptual truncations.

To understand and appreciate Eastern Psychology requires that one suspend the cultural beliefs and values with which we have been inculcated as modern Westerners, particularly while first studying the basic ideas. Later, one may learn to appreciate the contributions of both Eastern and Western psychology, and to see that they are complementary rather than mutually exclusive.

It is also highly important to keep in mind while making an intellectual survey of Buddhist Psychology, the Zen caveat, "All teachings are no more than fingers pointing at the moon." This helps one to remember that the word is not the thing; the map is not the territory. An understanding of the deeper truths is achieved only through diligent and mindful individual practice. Simply memorizing words or slavishly adhering to practice guidelines produces little useful result.

There is, perhaps, no better place to begin the study of Buddhist Psychology than with the most basic teaching of the Buddha - *The Four Noble Truths*. The first three of these truths are:

1. There is suffering,

2. There is an identifiable cause of suffering, and

3. There is a path leading to the extinction of suffering.

So far these are not so different from ideas that can be found in Western Psychology/Psychotherapy. It may be useful to differentiate, at least for the initial discussion, two kinds of suffering - necessary suffering (suffering from injury, disease, old age, etc.) and unnecessary suffering (mental suffering that we create for ourselves out of ignorance of how our mind works). Ultimately, the distinction may be less important than it seems at first, but it is a tool that can help one make sense of what, initially, can seem like a paradoxical and often times opaque philosophical system.

The last of the Four Truths, which is the way to the extinction of suffering, is the called the *Eightfold Path.* The elements of this path are:

| 1. Right View | 5. Right Livelihood |
| 2. Right Thinking | 6. Right Diligence |
| 3. Right Speech | 7. Right Mindfulness |
| 4. Right Action | 8. Right Concentration |

While some may think of these as prescribed behaviors that precede and lead to enlightenment, it may be more useful to view them as concomitant with and stemming from growing realization of wisdom. Other aspects of Buddhist Psychology that will be addressed in the following paragraphs have a similar relationship to enlightenment, that is, they are not separate from it, but rather elements that grow with and are a part of it.

Fundamental to comprehending Buddhist Psychology is undertaking the practice that allows one to understand how one's own mind works. This fundamental practice is, of course, meditation. More specifically, the student must learn how to separate the internal observer (at times referred to as Big *M* mind, or mirror) from the discursive, or small *m* mind (the thinking, analyzing, planning, evaluating aspect of mind). This is important because, prior to awareness of it, it is the ongoing (often only semi-conscious) internal dialogue of the small *m* mind that generates and maintains our beliefs, feelings and behaviors, and thereby creates/perpetuates our suffering. Only unrelenting and dispassionate observation of the activities of the small *m* mind allows one to achieve awareness of this. Directly experiencing the small *m* mind from the position of the non-judging observer (the Big *M* mind) allows one to see past the veil of language and concepts, and experience the reality beyond.

An idea that separates Buddhism from most religions is the belief that everyone is already enlightened. Training does not produce a super-natural state, rather it uncovers an inherent quality or essence that is the birth right of every human. Enlightenment is sometimes referred to as awakening, which may be the most instructive way to describe it. (This is quite different from the Christian notion that humans are born into original sin and must be redeemed, and from the Freudian idea that life is an unending struggle between the Id, Ego and Super-Ego.)

The mind state in which the unrecognized internal dialogue creates an individual's reality is often referred to as *Samsara*, and in Eastern Psychology is generally considered to be the world of illusion. The world experienced by one who is free from the shackles of language and conditioned concepts is referred to as *Nirvana*. Nirvana is an ineffable experience, and the only way to know it is through a direct encounter. The enlightened being recognizes and accepts both Samsara and Nirvana as valid and meaningful. S/he is equally at home in each, and can choose to partake of either or both.

While the teachings (generally referred to in their written form as Sutras) provided by the Buddha and his antecedents and successors are clearly secondary in importance to the direct experience provided by meditation practice, they are helpful in understanding Buddhist Psychology. There are many teachings provided in the Sutras, too many to repeat here. So, instead of trying to be comprehensive, this introduction will consider the most significant subset of these that are generally held to be central to Buddhism and which help to explain Eastern Psychology.

The first idea is that of the *Five Aggregates* or *Skandhas*. These include our physical being (form), feelings, perceptions, mental formations and consciousness. The five aggregates contain everything, both inside and outside of us, in nature and in society. They are called aggregates because, although they may seem simple, unitary and separate at first glance, each is composed of many elements. For example, our physical being has many different systems that all contribute to its continued functioning. But beyond this, we contain genetic material that was also in our ancestors. The mitochondria that power our cells are separate but symbiotic organelles. We are constantly taking in nutrients and oxygen from and giving waste products back to our environment. In the most profound sense, we are continuous with both the past and the environment.

Likewise, feelings and perceptions have many elements. Feelings are generated by perceptions of events in our environment, the belief systems through which they are filtered, and the resulting thoughts we have about these perceived events. Perceptions are the limited and filtered data that is relayed to our brain by our sensory organs. Perceptions are also influenced by the conscious and unconscious concepts that are the product of our conditioning.

According to the Vijnanavada School of Buddhist thought, there are fifty-one categories of mental formations. The potential for each type of mental formation is present in all of us, though any particular formation may remain unmanifested at any given time. Some are wholesome, some are not. All are creations of our minds, are impermanent and without any real substance. It is these mental formations that are the primary objects of meditation. As one transforms consciousness, one also transforms unhealthy mental formations into healthy mental formations.

The seventh book of the Abhidharma, called the Pattana, describes the eighteen types of conditioning, including association and habit. This theory not only tells us how our minds become conditioned, thus forming an important aspect of Eastern Psychology, it also provides us with information on how to overcome the conditioning and the ignorance it creates so that we can move past it to unobstructed consciousness. Consciousness, as noted above, has two main aspects. While Big *M* mind, being unconditioned, is relatively simple, small *m* mind has many components, and is the product of much conditioning.

The second set of ideas to be considered are termed The Three Dharma Seals. These three are *Impermanence, Non-Self,* and *Nirvana*. The notion of Impermanence is just what it appears to be. The problem is that we often forget that everything is impermanent. We often try to keep things the same, and, in doing so, create suffering. Accepting and embracing change is essential to the resolution of suffering.

Non-Self is a somewhat more difficult concept to understand and accept. Western sensibilities and psychology assume a separate and enduring entity that is the core of each individual. Admonitions such as "be yourself" and "love yourself" encourage us to identify, enhance and protect the (illusory) entity that we identify as our "Self". Yet when observed deeply, we find that Self is just a concept which changes over time and is neither separate nor permanent. A metaphor that is often used to help us understand this concept is that of the wave realizing that it is simply water which is continuous with the rest of the ocean - that the characteristics of any particular wave are superficial, temporary, and created (conditioned) by its environment. Much of the suffering we experience comes from our involvement in defending our concept of our "Self". While the idea of Non-Self may seem nihilistic to some, it is not. Rather, it is the realization of this idea that allows us to finally feel fully connected to the rest of creation. Zen Master Dogen told us that "To study Zen is to study the Self. To study the Self is to forget the Self. To forget the Self is to be enlightened by the ten thousand things."

Finally, the term Nirvana can be understood as that state in which one has penetrated to that place beyond all conditioning - beyond language, beyond feelings, beyond concepts - to the state of pure direct experience. Concepts are finally understood to exist only as useful fictions - beneficial in certain circumstances, but having no ultimate validity. Understanding the three Dharma Seals is an element of wisdom, and is concomitant with *Non-Attachment* - an essential aspect of ending suffering, and with *Compassion* - complete empathy and the acceptance of all things just as they are.

The third set of ideas is referred to as the Three Doors of Liberation. These are *Emptiness, Signlessness*, and *Aimlessness.* Emptiness may be interpreted in two different ways. Thich Nhat Hanh construes it to mean empty of a separate existence. This is to say that each seemingly separate object we perceive is actually no more than an aspect of the flow that is all things. Thich Nhat Hanh refers to this as Interbeing or Interpenetration. In this sense, the concept of Emptiness is very similar to the ideas that created the fields of Ecology and Physics - the inseparable interrelatedness of all entities and systems. In another sense that one might derive from nuclear physics, Emptiness could also refer to the "empty" reality underlying the illusion of solidity and quiescence of macroscopic matter created by subatomic energy fields.

The notion of Signlessness is one that helps us see that how things appear is not necessarily their essence. Water can be a liquid, a solid or a gas, yet none of these is its essence. What we apprehend through our five senses is not ultimate reality. It is one aspect of reality, namely that part of reality that is created by the interaction of our senses and external "stuff". But because our senses were designed for a specific purpose - enhancing our chances to survive and thrive - they therefore exclude most data that is not important to our survival, and, therefore, do not provide us with an accurate picture of "reality".

The idea of Aimlessness encourages us to recognize that in the pursuit of ultimate knowledge, there is nothing to be achieved. We are already where we need to be. We only need to wake up and realize it. This is not the same as being lazy or failing to act out of fear. Rather it is recognizing that we must let go of the obfuscating debris of conditioned thought.  Through acquiring Aimlessness one gains non-attachment, humility and freedom from worry.

The fourth teaching is the Theory of Root Relations.  This theory states that all (mental) suffering can be traced to **Greed, Hatred** and **Delusion**.  Thus, one way to think about the release from suffering is to recognize these unhealthy roots, and allow them to be transformed into their opposites - generosity (***Non-Attachment***), empathy (***Compassion***), and clarity (***Enlightenment***).

The foregoing discussion is hardly a comprehensive discussion of Buddhist Psychology.  It may, however, give the reader a glimpse of how Buddhist practitioners and scholars have thought about human psychology.  But, paradoxically, this intellectual discourse only serves to create more concepts which will ultimately need to be given up.  Thus they are, at best, the proverbial and metaphorical raft useful only to carry one to the other shore - to that land beyond all conceptual thought.

It is more than a little interesting to note that important aspects of these concepts first enunciated in ancient India reappear in the lore of Yaqui Indian brujos, and, in an only slightly altered form, in modern Western Psychology e.g., cognitive-behavioral psychotherapy. Such convergence should not go unnoticed. To quote the old aphorism, The more things change, the more they stay the same.

It is the hope of the author that what the reader will take away from the above is a clear understanding that Eastern Psychology is psychology. It is not religion; it is not mysticism; it is not spiritualism. It is psychology, and its principal components are constructs that are consistent with many of those found in Western Psychology. In fact, Eastern Psychology is the first systematic presentation of cognitive-behavioral psychology. One has only to review the prescriptions of the Eightfold Path to confirm this. There is nothing mystical or religious about the five aggregates. Nor is there anything mystical or religious about the notions of impermanence, non-self, or nirvana. We all know that things change; Charles Cooley and George Herbert Mead long ago identified the superficial and transitory aspects of what we call self; and Nirvana is nothing more than the experience of the unconditioned mind.

The Four Noble Truths are about attachment, or as we currently term it, addiction. The concept of addiction is generally accepted and widely used. However, most mental health professionals - in fact, most people - prefer to apply the term to others. Just as alcoholics are often in denial about their addiction to alcohol, most Westerners are in denial about their addiction to wealth, to fossil fuels, to privilege, etc., and to the myths that support these addictions.

We have already discussed at length the explanations of Emptiness and Signlessness that are proffered by modern physics, studies of perception, and analyses of language. Here again, there is nothing of religion or mysticism. The idea of Aimlessness is a little more difficult for most people in that it appears to contradict the Protestant Ethic. As long as one holds on to the idea that s/he is defined by his/her wealth or achievements, the idea of aimlessness is anathema. And while accepting aimlessness may be difficult for most people, it is not a religious or mystical issue; it is a psychological issue.

And who will try to argue that greed, hatred and delusion are religious or mystical. These are so clearly issues for psychology that it is hard to imagine any mental health professional suggesting otherwise. Is there any mental health professional out there who would not support generosity, empathy and mental clarity? There is nothing vague or ephemeral in any of these concepts. They are immediate, concrete and relevant.

When Galileo first presented his heliocentric theory it was rejected because it exceeded the capacity of most of his contemporaries to understand. It took them far out of their comfort zone. And it challenged the authority of the Roman Catholic Church. Although we all (or at least most of us) now accept that the sun is the center of the solar system, and our planetary system is only a tiny handful of pebbles at the outer edge of a huge galaxy, such ideas were beyond the ability of sixteenth century minds to fathom. Likewise, many of the ideas that sprang from the theory of relativity and from quantum mechanics strained even the greatest minds of the time. Even now, most humans remain unaware of these ideas, and would find them difficult or impossible to accept if presented with them.

These problems are virtually identical with the ones facing Eastern Psychology. It is a difficult set of ideas for many to understand because some of the terms are metaphorical and beyond the comprehension of those who have not experienced deep meditative states or even strange and unfamiliar cultures. But the problem is not with those who have undertaken the training, experienced the results and shared their experiences. It is with those who critique through the lenses of ignorance, never having experienced the ineffable. The solution is in looking beyond one's limitations, and addiction to power. The current position of the Western Psychological Establishment considering Eastern Psychology is, in some respects, not unlike the position of the seventeenth century Roman Catholic Church facing the challenge posed by Galileo. Let us hope that it will not take as long for Eastern Psychology to be recognized as it took heliocentric theory

# Interlinear

"Please tell me, don Juan, what exactly is controlled folly?" Don Juan laughed loudly and make a smacking sound by slapping his thigh with the hollow of his hand.

"This is controlled folly!" he said, and laughed and slapped his thigh again.

"What do you mean . . . ?"

"I am happy that you finally asked me about my controlled folly after so many years, and yet, it wouldn't have mattered to me in the least if you had never asked, Yet I have chosen to feel happy, as if I cared, that you asked, as if it would matter that I care. That is controlled folly!

"I told you once that our lot as men is to learn, for good or bad," he said. "I have learned to see, and I tell you that nothing really matters; now it is your turn; perhaps some day you will see, and you will know then whether things matter or not. For me nothing matters, but perhaps for you everything will. You should know by now that a man of knowledge lives by acting, not by thinking about acting, not by thinking about what he will think when he has finished acting. A man of knowledge chooses a path with a heart and follows it; and

131

*then he looks and rejoices and laughs; and then he sees and knows. He knows that his life will be over altogether too soon; he knows, because he sees, that nothing is more important than anything else. In other words, a man of knowledge has no honor, no dignity, no family, no name, no country, but only life to be lived, and under these circumstances his only tie to his fellow man is his controlled folly.*

*"Thus a man of knowledge endeavors, and sweats, and puffs, and if one looks at him he is just like any ordinary man, except that the folly of his life is under control. Nothing being more important than anything else, a man of knowledge chooses any act, and acts it out as if it matters to him. His controlled folly makes him say that what he does matters and makes him act as if it did, and yet he knows that it doesn't; so when he fulfills his acts he retreats in peace, and whether his acts were good or bad, or worked or didn't, is in no way part of his concern.*

*"A man of knowledge may choose, on the other hand, to remain totally impassive and never act, and behave as if to be impassive really matters to him; he will be rightfully true at that too, because that would also be his controlled folly."*

**Carlos Castaneda** - *A Separate Reality*

# Chapter 8

## A New Framework

"... no experience is definable without a logical framework ...

Any apparent disharmony can be removed only by

an appropriate widening of the conceptual framework."

**Niels Bohr**

*Atomic Theory &Human Knowledge*

The history of humankind is full of transitions in beliefs about the nature of our world and our place in it. What was once a flat earth is now a sphere. A geocentric faith has been transformed into heliocentric postulate. Newtonian physics have been subsumed by the theory of relativity. And the notion of a fixed objective reality has been replaced by the recognition of a neo-solipsistic interpretation of the "out there". What is most interesting about this last transition is that it involves an understanding arrived at by a "religious" tradition whose lineage goes back thousands of years, and which has been confirmed by the highest level of modern science and linguistic analysis. Perhaps there is to come yet another transition which remains veiled in the mists of the future. But, given the fact that our consciousness is still stuck in three dimensions, we remain blind to what may be the next realization or when it will come. However, this should not prevent us from utilizing all current understanding to maximize the possibility of future advances.

In his thoughtful volume, *The Structure of Scientific Revolutions*, Thomas Kuhn (1962) proposes that under the usual circumstances science "progresses" by working out the unsolved problems posed by the existing scientific worldview or paradigm. By paradigm he means "the coherent traditions of scientific research", which are derived from models provided by, "examples of actual scientific practice - examples of which include law, theory, application and instrumentation together." (p. 10)

A revolution in science, i.e., a change in paradigm, typically occurs when anomalies are discovered which cannot be resolved within the existing paradigm. For anomalies to have any effect on the course of events they first have to be noticed and given credence. It is not easy for this to occur since the paradigm for any science does so much to determine what observations are made, how they are made, and how the results are analyzed and interpreted. Generally speaking, it is easier to ignore anomalies or to claim that they are only apparent anomalies that will eventually be correctly understood and fit into the existing framework, than to undertake a change of paradigm.

Modern physics is a classic example of a paradigm shift. Relativity theory was rejected for many years by a large number of physicists. Eventually, as the evidence mounted and the predictions generated by the theory were borne out in practice, virtually all of the holdouts capitulated, and Newtonian physics was superseded by relativity and quantum physics. A full and coherent description of the phenomena of the universe was simply beyond the capacity of the Newtonian mode.

With regard to psychology, the only existing paradigm for most of the past four millennia was that generated by the sages of the East. Looked at from the perspective of this time frame, as well as a more global viewpoint, modern Western psychology is only in its infancy. Its dominance in the Western world is due, in significant measure, to a general ignorance of, and /or disdain for, Eastern traditions.

But, given the fact that the West has become increasingly aware of the East, and that physics has shown the limitations of reductionism and objectivity, we need to reintroduce Eastern theory and method to supplement Newtonian psychology. While Newtonian psychology can provide much useful information just as Newtonian physics has, it cannot effectively address the questions that are posed in "Relativity" psychology any more than Newtonian theory can address the issues of Einsteinian physics. Given the circumstances, it appears that the field of psychology is in need of a shift in its paradigm. Our old notions of reality - materialistic, deterministic, reductionistic and time-independent space - have been shown by modern physics to be limited in their applicability. What we believed to be the fundament of reality has turned out to be only one of the many forms it might take. And that form was determined by the various filters that stand between our conscious awareness and the "out there". It is, perhaps, time that we recognized and accepted that all experience is

136

ultimately subjective, and consider the advantages of the expansion of method in the field of psychology.

It is the purpose of the present chapter to propose that psychology consider legitimizing the psychological ideas and methods set forth in Eastern wisdom - a position some would call anti-scientific. I suggest that we think of such a more inclusive discipline as "extra-scientific". It has not hurt the position of those advocating change that physicists from Capra back down the line have confirmed the crossover between physics and Eastern Psychology; that these ancient ideas are seen to correspond with the results of "experiments of great precision and sophistication, and on a rigorous and consistent mathematical formalism." (Capra, 1975, p. 19)

The acceptance of Relativistic Psychology will allow us to reconsider our notions about ultimate mental health as Walsh and Shapiro (1983) have done in their exemplary and fascinating volume. We can expand on the notions that Erich Fromm put forth in *The Sane Society* and *Escape From Freedom*. Relativistic Psychology allows us to explore consciousness through consciousness and thereby address the subjective component of consciousness in a quasi-objective manner (i.e., utilizing group consensus). We can thereby address the issues of ultimate "sanity" and the experiential qualities of the various states of consciousness including the "fourth" state identified in the Yogic tradition.

It may be useful at this juncture to pause for a moment and consider a linguistic dichotomy that creates a great deal of mischief. I speak of the notion of the incompatibility of science and religion which some may wish to impose on this discussion. While it is true that religious leaders of both the past and present have disagreed with the methods and findings of science, and declared "faith" outside of and unchallengeable by science, this has not been true of spokesmen for Buddhism. As the Dalai Lama (2005) points out so lucidly in his book, *The Universe in a Single Atom*, Buddhism finds no conflict in embracing science as a complementary and very important path to knowledge. And, almost half a century earlier, D.T. Suzuki (1960), one of the most respected spokesmen of Zen in the West remarked, "Zen, however, we must remember, has no objection whatever to the scientific approach to reality; Zen only desires to tell scientists that theirs is not the only approach." ( p. 30)

That our experience of the world is ultimately a relative and subjective - albeit often a highly functional - one, is now indisputable.   While this fact may have relatively minor consequences for some of the physical sciences, for others, particularly psychology, its implications are significant.   In the most basic sense, all scientific knowledge is created, as much as it is discovered.   But, even though objectivity as it has been conceived in the past simply cannot be, it does not mean that our existing conceptual maps are no longer of any use.   Because many of them have proved themselves of great value in a pragmatic sense, we would be foolish to completely divest ourselves of them.   And yet, it is also important to remember that they are maps and not the territory.

For psychology, the ultimately subjective nature of all experience has a double implication.   Not only must psychologists, like other students of science, accept the "useful fiction" nature of their findings and theories, they must also embrace subjective experience as a major area of study. Further, psychologists must adopt or develop methods of study appropriate to the subject matter.   To deny this or to avoid dealing with it is as absurd as looking out in the street for a key lost on the doorstep.

If the evidence is so clear cut and overwhelming as I have proposed, why has not mainstream psychology already taken the steps necessary to institute a change? It is likely that there are at least several reasons why change is lagging. Like physicists before, practitioners of psychology are caught up in the current paradigm and are unlikely to change course without a large and compelling reason. In fairness, it must be acknowledged that the "objective empirical scientific method" has enjoyed considerable success in the natural sciences and many psychologists have enjoyed successful careers following this path. Given the strength of the current culture and the degree to which enculturated psychologists are rewarded for their adherence to existing norms, we should not have expected that they would be clamoring for change.

A second reason for resistance to embracing a new paradigm which includes use of "non-objective" approaches is the false belief that subjective methods are pseudoscience, and that subjective is the opposite and mutually exclusive pole on a single dimension. Thus, many psychologists believe that one must either espouse science and reject subjectivism, or accept subjective method and remain befuddled by the Dionysian chaos of raw experience. In point of fact, as noted earlier, the choice is not a battle of mutually exclusive entities.

In addition, there is probably a third, more personal, reason for reluctance to change. When individuals spend a substantial number of years learning how to do things in a particular fashion and in developing relationships based on these practices, they often have difficulty stepping outside of their acquired and nurtured frame of reference. Even if they are willing to open themselves up to a new possibility, commitment written in years of practicing and teaching a particular point of view is not easily discarded and replaced. The irony is that the very method that could be used to dispel the rigidity of such conditioning is the very method they wish to exclude from consideration as a legitimate epistemology.

However, given the momentum started in physics, and psychology's area of study, the transition to a more inclusive paradigm is probably inevitable, despite the cultural opposition. As Theodore Roszak (1969) has stated, "What is to blame is the root assumption, . . . [namely] that culture - if it is to be cleansed of superstition and reclaimed for humanitarian values - must be wholly entrusted to the mindscape of scientific rationality. I have insisted that there is something radically and systematically wrong with our culture . . . which frustrates our best efforts to achieve wholeness. I am convinced that it is our ingrained commitment to the scientific picture of nature that hangs us up."

With the advent of the new culture of modern physics, the landscape has, however, begun to change, and the overall direction is toward the more inclusive framework.

The new framework herein proposed is really quite simple. It consists of two basic propositions: 1.) That the ultimately subjective nature of all knowledge, in psychology as elsewhere, be formally acknowledged, and that the study of subjective experience by the most appropriate methods be accepted as having full and equal status with all other areas of psychology; and 2.) That the various theoretical positions in psychology be recognized as the useful fictions - or maps, if you will - that they are, and that the relationship of the different types of study be considered as complementary rather than as competitive or mutually exclusive.

Approaches to studying directly the subjective aspect of human experience have already germinated. Clearly the traditions of Eastern Psychology, and perhaps the work of those studying non-ordinary reality, provide piers from which to embark. Ornstein (1977), for example, in his *Psychology of Consciousness* has presented ideas regarding a new direction based on the philosophies of the Orient in a brief but comprehensible form along with some cogent arguments as to why these methods should become tools of contemporary psychological practice. Likewise, Charles Tart (1975) has proposed a systems approach to the study of consciousness which includes the notion of state-specific sciences, although he too borrows substantially form the philosophies of the Orient.

An example of an area in which the methods and ideas stemming from the Buddhist/meditation tradition might be useful is the study of the concept of self. When most people think of "self", they think of the unique and unchanging aspect of their conscious experience that has continuity over time via memories, resides primarily within the confines of their skin, and is identified as "me". When a person is asked to describe his or her "self" he/she will typically provide a list of attributes including such items as what he/she does for a living, his/her interests, his/her physical attributes, age, gender, values and beliefs. These descriptions are parts of stories people tell themselves about who they are.

Social scientists have been prone to look at the "self" as a social construction. Charles Cooley (McIntyre, 2005) formulated the notion of the "looking-glass self", i.e. a story about who one is generated from the verbal and non-verbal input of significant others in one's environment. Inherent in the idea of "self" as a social construction is the acknowledgment that the "self" changes over time. But this raises a problem, namely, how much can a "self" change and still be the same "self"? And what about multiple personalities? Which is their real "self"?

The problem is probably at least partly one of semantics. Linguists remind us that language is simply as set of arbitrary and conventionalized symbols. It is a map, and the map is *not* the territory. Words representing simple objects - cup, ball, dog, tree - generally do not cause much difficulty in communication. However, words representing concepts - religion, love, terrorist, eternity, and, yes, "self" - hold the potential for much greater ambiguity, and therefore for broad differences in meaning and interpretation. (There are even words, e.g., vampire, werewolf, that have no actual external referent.) To the extent that we think of a word as something having a location or qualities, we limit our ability to understand more subtle concepts.

As noted previously, one possible solution to the problem of understanding the concept of "self" comes from the tradition of meditation. Those who engage in the practice of meditation often differentiate between two different minds or, more precisely, two qualities of mind. Small *m* mind is that aspect of mind which makes grocery lists, schedules vacations, ponders where to seat eccentric Uncle Ned at the next Thanksgiving dinner, and balances the check book. Big *M* mind is that aspect of mind which, when developed, non-judgmentally observes all of one's thoughts, feelings and experiences.

Small *m* mind makes use of language and other symbolic conventions. Big *M* mind, on the other hand, which does not solve problems, take sides, or experience attraction or distaste, remains free from symbolic translation. It is, rather, pure awareness, and is sometimes referred to as unconditioned mind. It is the aspect of mind that does not change. Is it then conceivable that Big *M* mind is the essence or locus of the elusive sense of continuity that is "no-self"? Such a formulation may help to explain how, in the paradoxical logic of the Zen masters, "self" and "no self" can comfortably co-exist.

Other aspects of Buddhist psychology appropriate for study can be gleaned from the Abhidharma, and the commentaries on it. For example, the seventh book of the Abhidharma, the Pattana, lists 24 propositions that describe mental processes which can be combined to form a general theory.  In these propositions we find a model of mind that starts with sensory data, moves through the ways in which this data is processed and conditioned, and ends with a discussion of unconditioned, or non-dualistic, mind.

Specific propositions from the Abhidharma include the following ideas.  Our minds are full of images of objects that influence our thinking, feeling and action - sometimes without our conscious awareness.  Our "self" is one of these images, and, because of the distortions it contains, it is the source of much of our suffering.  The various images in one's mind develop associations with other images, and, any given image tends to trigger associated images, thus giving rise to a stream of thoughts and feelings.  These images and thoughts are interdependent, that is, none can exist without the other.  This mirrors the interdependence of objects in the physical world.

These mental images or states or beliefs become conditioned by various inducements (rewards or expected rewards).  Through cultivation and repetition these predispositions and beliefs become habitual.  We keep our conditioning going by "feeding" it.  Humans tend to reinforce that which is familiar, whether thoughts, feelings, behaviors or belief systems.  Our internal dialogue repeats and strengthens our beliefs, so that we ultimately become strongly attached to our views. This attachment is often subtle and sometimes unconscious, but it is the source of much suffering. Much of this is consistent with cognitive psychology and familiar to those who study it. Thus, integrating these aspects of Eastern and Western Psychology should not be difficult.

The Abhidharma goes on to discuss the theory of Karma - the law of moral consequence - which says that all deliberate actions ultimately create the seeds of future pleasant or unpleasant "fruit" according to their nature. The final sections of the Abhidharma discuss ways to "tame" the mind, and move beyond the conditioned to enlightenment. Paradoxically, enlightenment is not viewed as an achievement, but rather the result of surrendering and seeing the unconditioned mind that has always been there. Here again, we find ideas that have a familiar ring.

Perhaps the exploration of such concepts as mind, consciousness and creativity can benefit from utilizing the perspective of Eastern Psychology. Lest this be misunderstood, it is not the total replacement of current method that is being advocated. Rather, to refer back to the concerns expressed by

Sigmund Koch, that we tailor the method of inquiry to the subject matter.

The second aspect of change herein proposed is that psychological theories currently viewed as being in competition, be considered as complementary or as alternative maps of the territory of the human condition. Here again, the history of physics provides us with some food for thought. For some years, the wave and the corpuscular theories of the nature of light were considered by many to be in direct conflict, and it was expected that, with enough additional research, one would eventually triumph. However, Niels Bohr's realization that how one conceived of light depended on the conditions under which one studied it, led to the formulation of the principle of complementarity. This was an explicit recognition of the fact that we don't (and maybe can't) know the "true" nature of light, but only that it can manifest itself as either particles or waves.

Psychology is currently in a situation analogous to the pre-complementarity physics of light. Behaviorism, Humanism, Psychoanalysis, Analytic Psychology, etc. are viewed by many as being conflicting and competing theoretical positions. When considered from the truly subjectivist point of view, however, the conflict between the various theories (though perhaps not

148

their respective advocates) all but disappears. The theories are rightfully recognized as the creations of their authors, and as descriptive metaphors for a particular section of, or perspective on, human experience. They are, in a very fundamental sense, maps (some might call them useful fictions) that have varying degrees of utility; but, it is quite clear, none is the territory, much less, the entire territory.

The situation might be considered analogous to the conflict experienced by the blind persons who set out to study an elephant. One stumbled upon the trunk, and examined it thoroughly. Another found a tusk, a third the ear, a fourth the tail, and so forth. Thus, each thought they had found the essence of elephantness, and argued with his comrades about what constituted the true nature of the beast. It is only from our sighted vantage point that we are able to "see" that they were at once all right and all wrong.

Anyone who has studied Freud is aware of the degree to which his personal life and his socio-cultural circumstances shaped his theoretical perspective. But, is there anyone who would seriously contend that our parents are irrelevant to the course of our development, or that sexuality is a factor of only minor importance in human life? If we search deeply enough we will find that what is true of Freud and Psychoanalysis is also true for other psychologists and their theories.

The fact that different theorists have focused on different phenomena, e.g., past trauma, history of conditioning, cognitive structures, personality types or traits, unconscious drives, etc., in their respective searches for the "causes" of behavioral or psychological events has certainly helped to make their products appear contradictory. That each has carved up the phenomena observed in a different manner, and generated a new set of terms for naming the resulting segments, has undoubtedly added to the confusion and appearance of mutual exclusivity. But, ultimately, the choice of what part of the elephant to study and the words created to describe the chosen part is subjective.

Potentially useful models for integrating existing psychological perspectives have already been suggested by at least two authors. It is worth noting that both have started with a framework derived from Eastern religious philosophy and shown how contemporary Western psychological theories can be included. Joseph Campbell, the noted mythologist, has proposed that the chakra system of Kundalini Yoga can easily incorporate the major Western psychological theoretical positions (Campbell, 2003). Chakras, which in the Yogic tradition represent different levels of functioning and consciousness, are often represented as residing at different levels of the human spine, with the chakra at the base of the spine representing the fundamental survival aspects of experience. Campbell opines that this chakra is one for which a behavioral psychology is most fitting. The next higher chakra, which is associated with sexual energy and emotion, is one for which a Psychoanalytic psychology would be appropriate. Each succeeding higher chakra requires a different set of parameters (and terms) for understanding and exploring. The seventh, or Crown, chakra, is the metaphorical space in which one can experience union with the divine. Due to the inevitably ineffable nature of the experience and subject matter, language will, of necessity, be inexact and highly metaphorical.

Campbell points out that both the Eastern and Western traditions benefit from this marriage. The Yogic system gains from the intensive study and articulation of the Western psychologies on the subject matter of the lower chakras. The Western theories benefit through seeing their relationship to each other, and through realizing that there is more to be explored beyond the bounds of their own circumscribed and limited parameters.

Psychologists Daniel Goleman and Mark Epstein (1983), in discussing Eastern and Western Psychologies, state that, "The paradigms of traditional Asian psychologies, however, are capable of encompassing the major categories of contemporary [Western] psychology as well as this other mode of consciousness." (p. 250)

Using Tibetan Buddhism as a model, Goleman and Epstein explain and illustrate their assertion. "The Tibetan Wheel of Life, for example, depicts pictorially six realms of existence, each a metaphor for a different psychological state. One realm, the 'stupid beast', stands for the level of behavior which is totally conditioned, and corresponds to the world studied by Behaviorism, where habit and simple stimulus-response is the principle determinant of action and thought. The hell realms represent aggression and anxiety states, and are emblematic of all anxiety-based behavior; this is the realm of psychopathology as mapped by contemporary psychologists like Freud, Sullivan and Laing. The realm of *pretas,* or hungry ghosts, corresponds to insatiable appetite or needfulness - what Maslow has characterized as 'deficiency motivation'. The realm of heaven depicts god-like beings who represent sensual bliss and gratification of the highest order; the 'peak experience' would be subsumed by this category as would many of the experiences which have emerged from humanistic psychology." (p. 250)

In one sense, what I am proposing is that American psychology go forward by looking to its roots; namely James' attention to "religious experience", and Titchener's use of introspection. Unfortunately, these channels of thought dried up as scientific psychology expanded. It is ironic that the very fountainhead of scientific psychology, physics, has provided the basis for yet another new direction back to the future. However, we should now recognize that this is not an either-or situation. Both models and their methods have a legitimate place in contemporary psychology. A significant task for contemporary psychologists will be to determine future directions for research, and where to best employ each methodology.

# Chapter 9

## Some Practical Implications

In the pursuit of learning, every day something is acquired.

In the pursuit of Tao, every day something is dropped.

**Tao Te Ching (48)**

Any attempt to identify all the implications of a change in paradigm is bound to fall short of the mark. However, the fact that there are implications that are now apparent needs to be acknowledged and an accounting made. There are at least three areas of Western Psychology where the implications are significant:

1. The way in which we go about defining mental health,

2. The practice of psychotherapy, and

3. Research methodology.

Perhaps the most obvious area in which change is indicated is in how we think about and define mental health. Erich Fromm (1955) wrote about the "pathology of normalcy" and the "pathogenic function of modern society". Walsh and Shapiro (1983) noted that in the area of mental health, the focus of Western Psychology has been almost entirely on psychopathology. They further observe that, while Western Psychology has made substantial progress in understanding psychopathology, there has been a corresponding lack of attention to defining psychological health as it develops beyond the absence of psychopathology. They therefore attempt to open up the discussion on mental health by examining the ideas of those - particularly from the Eastern traditions - who have provided accounts of exceptional mental health. And with the current momentum toward acknowledging and even celebrating cultural diversity, it is somewhat surprising that academic psychology has not already embraced the psychology of other cultures. Psychologists, above all others, should recognize the importance and value of reaching out across cultural and national boundaries in the service of enhancing international understanding and empathy, as well as augmenting our own understanding.

To the extent that we continue to define mental health as simply the absence of psychopathology (as defined in the DSM), we abdicate our responsibility to provide criteria for, and paths to, a standard of mental health that exceeds mere cultural conformities and the limitations of the consciousness filters identified in previous chapters.    Just as Western medicine has begun to integrate non-traditional ideas and practices such as acupuncture, herbal medicine and meditation, psychology needs to soften its defenses against alternative psychologies.

One very simple example of the nature of, and path toward, positive mental health is embodied in the quotation from the Tao Te Ching cited at the beginning of the chapter.  While the Western notion of mental health focuses on learning more "stuff", and on increasing the amount of knowledge an individual has, the Eastern view is almost the complete opposite.  "In pursuit of the Tao, everyday something is dropped."  But here we must remind ourselves of the significance of Eastern paradoxical logic.  The road to exceptional mental health does NOT require that one forget everything one has learned.  Rather, one must recognize the learning, i.e., the conditioning, for what it is, and learn to "see" into the space that exists outside of conditioning, and outside of culture.

A second, and arguably equally important area for integrating Eastern Psychology is the field of psychotherapy. It needs to be said at the outset that psychotherapy like the rest of psychology is a diverse group of theories and practices. Psychoanalytic, Analytic, Humanistic, Gestalt, Existential, Behavioral, Cognitive-Behavioral, etc. - all are psychotherapeutic approaches widely practiced today. To be thorough and fair, it must be acknowledged that Christian and Buddhist orientations have already made significant inroads into the practice of psychotherapy.

Attempts have been made in the past to compare and contrast disparate theoretical perspectives. Fromm, Suzuki and deMartino (1960) investigated Zen Buddhism and Psychoanalysis. Dollard and Miller (1950) explored the relationship between Psychoanalysis and learning theory. Alan Watts (1975) examined the various aspects of psychotherapy set forth in the Modern West and in Eastern Psychology. Since every theory employs a certain structural model and linguistic conventions, to some extent, the question is not so much which theory is right and which is wrong, but rather in what context and in what manner is each useful.

It has been largely the case that psychotherapy training has taken place in academic settings. Because of this, most psychotherapists have received training and indoctrination in the scientific paradigm. Alan Watts (1975) writes, "the psychotherapist carries on his work with an almost wholly unexamined 'philosophical unconscious'. He tends to be ignorant, by reason of his highly specialized training, not only of the contemporary philosophy of science, but also of the hidden metaphysical premises which underlie all the main forms of psychological theory. Unconscious metaphysics tend to be bad metaphysics. What if the metaphysical presuppositions . . . are invalid?" ( p. 26)

Often, this unconscious aspect of training prevents the psychotherapist from seeing that the problem an individual brings to therapy is often more than one of individual maladjustment. For example, studies such as the Midtown Manhattan Project (Srole, et al., 1962) have shown that over 80% of a large representative sample of urban dwellers showed symptoms of psychological impairment. On the basis of such evidence Watts notes that it is increasingly apparent that, "the normal state of consciousness in our culture is both the context and the breeding ground of mental illness." (p. 16)   This position is also embraced and extensively explored by Erich Fromm in his book, *The Sane Society*.

The fact that therapists often work with families and other types of groups, as well as individuals, indicates an awareness that individual pathology is often intimately intertwined with other elements of the social network.  The role of socio-cultural factors in mental illness goes even deeper than this, however. Further elaborating this point, Watts states, "what needs to be analyzed or clarified in an individual's behavior is the way in which it reflects the contradictions and confusions of the culture." (p. 27-8)  He includes in culture the "conventions of language and law, of ethics and aesthetics, of status, role and identity, and of cosmology, philosophy and religion.  For this whole social complex is what provides the individual's conception of himself, his state of consciousness, his very feeling of existence.  What is more, it provides the human organism's idea of its individuality.

"There are many reasons why distress comes from confusing this social [overlay] with reality.  There is direct conflict between what the individual organism is and what others say it is and expect it to be.  The rules of social communication often contain contradictions which lead to impossible dilemmas in thought, feeling, and action. Or it may be that confusion of oneself with a limiting and impoverished view of one's role or identity creates feelings of isolation, loneliness, and alienation. The multitudinous differences between individuals and their social context leads to as many ways of seeking relief from these conflicts. Some seek it in the psychoses and neuroses which lead to psychiatric treatment, but for the most part release is sought in the socially permissible orgies of mass entertainment, religious fanaticism, chronic sexual titillation, alcoholism, war - the whole sad list of tedious and barbarous escapes.

". . . the therapist who is really interested in helping the individual is forced into social criticism. This does not mean that he has to engage directly in political revolution: it means that he has to help the individual in liberating himself from the various forms of social conditioning, which includes liberation from hating this conditioning - hatred being a form of bondage to its object. The aim of [this sort of therapy] is not the destruction of [this social overlay] but seeing it for what it is, or seeing through it." (p. 20-22)

Psychotherapist David Brazier (1995), in his exposition on

Zen therapy, identifies the key to Buddhist thought and his use of Zen in therapy as the analysis of mental conditioning. "The aim of therapy," he states, "is to liberate the mind by enabling it to let go of the conditioned states." The "self" is the sum of all of our conditioning; therefore, true mental health is the result when one arrives at a state of "no-self" or "no-mind", that is, the state of pure, unconditioned awareness in which we find things just as they are, and each moment, we see our existence as the miracle that it truly is.

This is exactly the view that one working within the subjectivist framework would arrive at. Our reality, and the source of much misguided thinking, is the result of the interaction of our ontologically evolved being and the culturally/linguistically created internal dialogue. Since we are all "in" a culture, we all experience the delusion created by the cultural context. That one is adjusted to his/her culture is not necessarily an indication of health, nor is deviancy necessarily an indication of pathology. As Erich Fromm so cogently puts it in *The Sane Society*, the proper criteria of sanity are universal not cultural.

These comments are not intended to diminish the value or potential value of contemporary forms of Western psychotherapy. To the extent that they further an individual's progress on the road to understanding and diminishing unnecessary pain, they can be very valuable. But to the extent that they have culturally induced limitations, they are useful only to the edge of their limits. Typically, one must engage in a treatment or practice which goes beyond the limits of one's social conditioning to understand the nature and effects of social indoctrination, and to move beyond the conditioning in which we are stuck.

To build on an idea presented earlier, we might consider the role of "self" in psychotherapy. A typical goal in contemporary Western psychotherapy would be to explore a client's self-concept, and to work on replacing "negative" self-referents with positive ones. In other words, building self-esteem. While this might be an endpoint for Western therapy, a Buddhist therapist would view this as an important and useful but intermediate stage of treatment. Since ultimately these stories we tell ourselves about ourselves are, in fact, only stories, and are subject to change from many sources and influences, the solution to the "problem of self" is to move beyond the notion of "self" to "no self".

The ultimate goal of those designing psychotherapeutic

protocols should be to generate a model with multiple modalities and multiple paths that can accommodate all varieties of psychological dysfunction, and levels of problem resolution that culminates, for each and every patient, in the possibility of achieving what the masters of Eastern Psychology would call enlightenment or awakening. Any patient might choose to stop or pause at any level of accomplishment, but would know that further advancement was designed into the model, and was available to all.

The third major area of implication is methods of acquiring knowledge. Since the basis of the current critique is in physics and the scientific method, it is fitting that we begin our discussion there. Since it is now clear that all experience, scientific as well as the rest, is ultimately subjective, it is essential that psychology formally adopt this as a tenet and expand its acceptable methodology to include, at least provisionally, methods used by those who have explored non-ordinary states of reality.

A method of knowing used since the dawn of recorded history is meditation. The worldview generated from experiences with this method has not only withstood the test of time, it has now been confirmed by the hardest of the hard sciences. There are, however, several caveats to be noted in our consideration of this method of knowing. First, in the conventional Western sense, most meditation is not a religious practice, i.e., it is not focused around a belief in a supreme being or beings. The Four Noble Truths one studies as a Buddhist (Hanh, 1998) do not require that one be a theist. They simply explicate the Buddhist beliefs about human suffering and its cure. Meditation is, then, a method for exploring for oneself the "truths" propounded in the Sutras and similar teachings. Second, there are a variety of different practices loosely grouped under the general rubric of meditation. Some people use meditation as a way to relax; others use it as a way to gain various powers (siddhis) including conscious control of autonomic functions; others still, as a way of focusing attention on certain subjects. The meditation practice which is of primary interest here, however, is the type used by Zen practitioners or those who practice mindfulness meditation. This type of meditation involves noticing the thoughts and feelings that arise while one sits, and, without evaluating or dismissing them, bringing attention back to the present time and place, the here and now.

According to the literature, and the reports of those who are experienced practitioners, this practice sometimes produces non-ordinary states of consciousness. The knowledge derived from these states is confirmed by consensus of those who have experienced it, and now, by the findings of physics, physiology and linguistics. There are, in addition to these meditation-induced states of non-ordinary reality, other states of non-ordinary reality generated by other practices. Entheogens such as peyote, psilocybin mushrooms, ayahuasca, and soma, as well as the fasting/contemplation components of the vision quest, have all been reliably reported to produce states of non-ordinary reality from which important information is imparted.

It appears unlikely that states such as these can be studied and understood using only the existing methodology employed by mainstream psychologists. A new methodology must be employed. Some may argue that Structuralism's method of Introspectionism has been tried and rejected by psychology as inadequate. However, since Zen meditation differs from Introspectionism, and given the change in knowledge and perspective since the demise of Structuralism, it seems reasonable to look anew at what was formerly considered to be too subjective for real science.

Since many Western psychologists are still unfamiliar with

the meditative method, there will undoubtedly be some groping in darkness as Western psychologists work toward ways of talking about, understanding and categorizing the data acquired by this method. Although it can no longer be argued successfully that other approaches are strictly empirical while this is not, the unfamiliarity of the type of data and methods of analysis will, at least initially, pose some problems.

It is only prudent to recognize that any transition involving a new method of research and retraining in this method will involve a certain amount of resistance. However, this is no reason to stall the evolution to a more inclusive and potentially fruitful discipline. Just as it takes time and patience to train budding scientists about the importance of good research design and statistical analysis, so it will take time to retrain existing practitioners how to add a new way of thinking and a new method to their existing library.

There is yet a fourth implication, or set of implications of the proposed framework, but it is somewhat more abstract than the three previously discussed. This framework and the findings on which it is based may be of help in providing new ways of thinking about old issues. The beauty and significance of Eastern Psychology is that it not only permits, but actually draws attention to and celebrates, the paradoxical nature of existence, and the ineffable nature of ultimate reality. It points directly to the fact that we can and should come to recognize both the ineffable and effable realities of our lives, and the logically contradictory state of affairs this creates, and learn not only to accept it, but to affirm it.

This includes such logical contradictions as idealism vs. materialism, free will vs. determinism, and one we have already addressed, subjectivity vs. objectivity. Our new framework suggests that these apparent dilemmas or contradictions may well be no more than a cultural/linguistic convention or "trap" (some might call it a koan) that simply obscures the solution which becomes clear once one is free of the culturally-linguistically imposed limitations. Just as we can understand objectivity as nothing more than a special case of the universally subjective nature of experience, so, other conflicts may be resolved in unexpected ways upon reconsideration in a larger framework.

The free will vs. determinism dilemma, for example, will eventually be recognized as a non-issue and put to rest. While we all experience causality (the handmaiden of determinism) in our daily lives, and can demonstrate regularities in the physical world, the concept breaks down at the subatomic level as does the concept of determinism at the experiential level. And we always run aground when we try to identify the cause of the universe. When describing human actions, we can often identify causes or antecedent conditions that contribute to various human actions. It would not make sense to totally give up the notion that one's past and history of conditioning are important in determining future choices and behavior. Yet no one has yet generated and replicated perfect correlations between past experience and future behavior.

Free will is also a useful concept. Almost everyone has experienced the discomfort of having to make a difficult choice; of being caught on the horns of a dilemma. Perhaps this is the experiential equivalent of having an identically powerful history of conditioning for each of two different potential responses. But in a world where there are so many environmental influences and so many intrapsychic factors, it is probably impossible to specify all the elements in a history of conditioning that contribute to even very simple decisions. Humans will always *experience* freedom of choice, and so it will always be a useful concept.

If we go one step further and accept the four-dimensional

space-time universe posited by physicists, in which time is the fourth dimension of space, then past, present and future already all exist side by side simultaneously, and the problem itself becomes meaningless.

There are undoubtedly many other implications of the paradigm shift I am proposing. However, it is beyond the scope of this brief volume to generate a comprehensive list of future directions for psychology. What I hope is now clear to the reader is that there are important and useful alternatives to Western concepts of psychology, and that acknowledging their existence and utility is necessary in order for the field to move forward. Holding fast to ideas and methods that are clearly limiting, for whatever reasons, is no longer defensible. We would do well to recall Emerson's statement that a foolish consistency is the hobgoblin of little minds.

# REFERENCES

## CHAPTER 1

Capra, F. (1975) *The Tao of Physics*. Berkeley, CA: Shambala.

Clark, R., (1971) *Einstein: The Life and Times*. New York: World Publishing Co.

Gould, S. (1977) *Ever Since Darwin*. New York: Norton.

Koch, S. (1959-1963) *Psychology: A Study of a Science*. New York: McGraw Hill.

Koch, S. (1969) Psychology cannot be a coherent science. *Psychology Today*, 3(4), 64-68.

Ornstein, R. (1977) *The Psychology of Consciousness (2nd Ed.)* New York: Harcourt, Brace Jovanovich..

Ouspensky, P. (1945) *Tertium Organum ($3^{rd}$ American Ed.).* New York: Knopf.

171

Wertheimer, M. (1972) *Fundamental Issues in Psychology.*
New York: Holt, Rinehart & Winston.


## CHAPTER 2


Boring, E. (1950) *A History of Experimental Psychology.*
(2nd Ed.) New York: Appleton.

Brazier, D. (1995) *Zen Therapy.* New York: John Wiley &
Sons.

Fromm, E. (1950) *Psychoanalysis and Religion.* New Haven:
Yale University Press.

Goleman, D. (1983) Meditation and well-being, in Walsh, R. &
Shapiro, D. *Beyond Health and Normality.* New York: Van
Nostrand Reinhold Company.

James, W. (1958) *The Varieties of Religious Experience.* New
York: Mentor.

Koch, S. (1969) Psychology cannot be a coherent science.
*Psychology Today, 3(4),* 64-68.

Metzner, R. (1971) *Maps of Consciousness*. New York: MacMillan.

Ornstein, (1977) *The Psychology of Consciousness (2nd Ed.)*. New York: Harcourt, Brace Jovanovich.

Smolin, L. (2006) *The Trouble with Physics*. Boston: Houghton Mifflin Company.

Watson, J. (1913) *Psychology as the Behaviorist Views It*. New York:

Watts, A. (1975) *Psychotherapy East and West*. New York: Vintage.

# CHAPTER 3

Bohr, N. (1934) *Atomic Physics and The Description of Nature*. Cambridge, GB: Cambridge University Press.

Capra, F. (1975) *The Tao of Physics*. Berkeley: Shambala.

Clark, R. (1971) *Einstein: The Life and Times*. New York: World Publishing Co.

Ouspensky, P. (1945) *Tertium Organum (3d American Ed.).* New York: Knopf.

Weyl, H. (1949) *Philosophy of Mathematics and Natural Science.* Princeton, NJ: Princeton University Press.

## CHAPTER 4

Ittelson, W. & Kirkpatrick, F. (1951) Experiments in perception. *Scientific American,* August, p. 50-55.

Jung, C. (1938) *Psychology and Religion (in Collected Works, vol. 11)* New Haven: Yale University Press.

Kohler, I. (1962) Experiments with goggles. *Scientific American,* May, p. 62-72.

Thomas, L, (1974) *Lives of a Cell.* New York: Viking Press.

## CHAPTER 5

Bagby, P. (1953) Culture and causes of culture. *American Anthropologist, 55(4),* 535-554.

Brown, N. (1959) *Life Against Death*. Middletown, CN: Wesleyan University Press.

Bohr, N. (1987) *Essays 1958-1962 on Atomic Physics and Human Knowledge*. Woodbridge, CN: Ox Bow Press.

Bruner, J. & Goodman, C. (1947) Value and need as organizing factors in perception. *Journal of Abnormal and Social Psychology, 42,* 33-44.

Capra, F. (1975) *The Tao of Physics*. Berkeley: Shambala.

Cassirer, E. (1944) *An Essay On Man*. New Haven: Yale University Press.

Castaneda, C. (1971) *A Separate Reality*. New York: Simon & Schuster.

Clark, R. (1971) *Einstein: The Life and Times*. New York: World Publishing Co.

Dundes, A. (1964) *Morphology of North American Indian Folktales*. New York: Pantheon.

Durrell, L (1961) *The Alexandria Quartet*. New York: Simon & Schuster

Ellson, D (1941) Experimental extinction of an hallucination produced by sensory conditioning. *Journal of Experimental Psychology, 28(4),* 350-361.

Huxley, A. (1956) *The Doors of Perception & Heaven and Hell*. New York: Harper & Row.

Klein, S. (1956-57) Zen Buddhism and general semantics. *ETC: A Review of General Semantics, 14(2),* 88-97.

Korzybski, A. (1958) *Science and Sanity: An Introduction to Non-Aristotelian Systems and general semantics. (2nd Ed.).* Lakeville, Conn.: International Non-Aristotelian Library.

Lee, D. (1950) Codifications of reality: Lineal and non-lineal. *Psychosomatic Medicine, 12(2)*

Polanyi, M. (1958) *Personal Knowledge: Towards a Post-Critical Philosophy*. Chicago: University of Chicago Press.

Tart, C. (1975) *States of Consciousness*. New York: Dutton.

Whorf, B. (1951) *Language, Thought and Reality: Selected Writings of Benjamin Lee Whorf.* (Ed. J.B. Carroll) Cambridge Mass: MIT Press.

Wittgenstein, L. (1953) *Philosophical Investigations.* Oxford: B. Blackwell.

# CHAPTER 6

Bridgeman, P. (1927) *The Logic of Modern Physics.* New York: Macmillan.

Campbell, D. & Fiske, D. (1959) Convergent and discriminant validation by the multitrait- multimethod matrix. *Psychological Bulletin, 56,* 81-105.

Koch, S. (1969) Psychology cannot be a coherent science. *Psychology Today, 3(4),* 64-68.

Marx, M & Hillix, W. (1963) *Systems and Theories in Psychology.* New York: McGraw-Hill.

Morison, R. (1960) Gradualness, gradualness, gradualness (I.P. Pavlov). *American Psychologist, 15,* 187-197.

Pelletier, K. (1977) *Mind As Healer, Mind As Slayer*. New York: Delacourt and Delta.

Plutchik, R (1968) *Foundations of Experimental Research*. New York: Harper & Row.

Watts, A. (1975) *Psychotherapy East and West*. New York: Vintage Books.

Wertheimer, M. (1972) *Fundamental Issues in Psychology*. New York: Holt, Rinehart & Winston.

# CHAPTER 7

Brazier, D. (1995) *Zen Therapy*. New York: John Wiley & Sons.

Capra, F. (1975) *The Tao of Physics*. Berkeley: Shambala.

Hanh, N. (1998) *The Heart of the Buddha's Teaching*. New York: Broadway Books.

Gabora, L (2010) Revenge of the "Neurds": Characterizing creative thought in terms of the structure and dynamics of memory. *Creativity Research Journal, 22(1)*, 1-13.

Horan, R. (2009) The neuropsychological connection between creativity and meditation. *Creativity Research Journal, 21(2-3)*, 199-222.

James, W. (1958) *Varieties of Religious Experience.* New Haven: Yale University Press.

Thera, N. (1998) *Abdhidhamma Studies.* Boston: Wisdom Publications.

Walsh, R. & Shapiro, S. (2006) The meeting of meditative disciplines and Western Psychology: A mutually enriching dialogue. *American Psychologist, 61(3)*, 227-239

# CHAPTER 8

Bohr, N. (1958) *Atomic Theory and Human Knowledge.* New York: John Wiley & Sons.

Campbell, J. (2003) *Myths of Light: Eastern Metaphors of the Eternal*. Novato, CA: New World Library.

Capra, F. (1975) *The Tao of Physics*. Berkeley: Shambala.

Dalai Lama (2005) *The Universe in a Single Atom*. New York: Morgan Road Books.

Fromm, E. (1941) *Escape From Freedom*. New York: Avon.

Fromm, E. (1955) *The Sane Society*. Greenwich, Conn.: Fawcett.

Goleman, D. (1983) Meditation and well-being. In Walsh, R & Shapiro, D. *Beyond Health and Normality*. New York: Van Nostrand Reinhold Company.

Kuhn. T. (1962) *The Structure of Scientific Revolutions*. Chicago: University of Chicago Press.

McIntyre, L. (2006) *The Practical Skeptic: Core Concepts in Sociology*. New York: McGraw Hill.

Ornstein, R. (1977) *The Psychology of Consciousness (2nd Ed.)*. New York: Harcourt, Brace, Jovanovich.

Roszak, T. (1969) *The Making of a Counterculture.* Garden City, NY: Doubleday.

Suzuki, D. (1960) Lectures on Zen Buddhism. In, Fromm, E., Suzuki, D. & deMartino, R. *Zen Buddhism and Psychoanalysis.* New York: Harper & Bros.

Tart, C. (1975) *States of Consciousness.* New York: Dutton.

Walsh, R. & Shapiro, D. (1983) *Beyond health and normality.* New York: Van Nostrand Reinhold Company.

## CHAPTER 9

Brazier, D. (1995) *Zen Therapy.* New York: John Wiley & Sons, Inc.

Dollard, J & Miller, N. (1950) *Personality and Psychotherapy.* New York: McGraw-Hill.

Fromm, E., Suzuki, D., & de Martino, R. (1960) *Zen Buddhism and Psychoanalysis.* New York: Harper & Brothers.

Fromm, E. (1955) *The Sane Society*. Greenwich, CN: Fawcett
  Publications.

Hanh, N. (1998) *The Heart of the Buddha's Teaching*. New
  York: Broadway Books.

Srole, L., et al. (1962) *Mental Health in the Metropolis: The
  Midtown Manhattan Study*. New York: McGraw-Hill.

Walsh, R. & Shapiro, D. (1983) *Beyond Health and Normality*.
  New York: Van Nostrand, Reinhold Company.

Watts, A. (1975) *Psychotherapy East and West*. New York:
  Vintage Books.